ALSO BY FAY THOMPSON

So Help Me God: The Whole Crazy Truth About Life, Creation, and Being Unapologetically You

Inspirations for a Brighter Day Volume I

Azez Medicine: Healing the Mind, Body, and Spirit With the Help of the Beings of the Light

INSPIRATIONS
for a Brighter Day

Volume II

FAY THOMPSON

Copyright © 2020 Fay Thompson
Cover Design: Fay Thompson
Published by: Big Moose Publishing
PO Box 127 Site 601 RR#6 Saskatoon, SK CANADA S7K3J9
www.bigmoosepublishing.com

All rights reserved. No part of this book may be used or reproduced by any means, graphic, electronic, or mechanical, including photocopying, recording, taping or by any information storage retrieval system without the written permission of the publisher except in the case of brief quotations embodied in critical articles and reviews.

Because of the dynamic nature of the Internet, any web addresses or links contained in this book may have changed since publication and may no longer be valid. The views expressed in this work are solely those of the author and do not necessarily reflect the views of the publisher, and the publisher hereby disclaims any responsibility for them.

The author of this book does not dispense medical advice or prescribe the use of any technique as a form of treatment for physical, emotional, or medical problems without the advice of a physician, either directly or indirectly. The intent of the author is only to offer information of a general nature to help you in your quest for emotional and spiritual well-being. In the event you use any of the information in this book for yourself, which is your constitutional right, the author and the publisher assume no responsibility for your actions.

ISBN 978-1-7752300-7-6 (paperback)
ISBN 978-1-989840-02-3 (ebook)

Big Moose Publishing 2/2020

For my big brother, Gary.

CONTENTS

ACKNOWLEDGEMENTS..*xvii*
HOW THIS BOOK CAME INTO BEING.........................*xix*
HOW TO USE THIS BOOK...*xxi*
ACCEPT HEAVEN'S HELP..1
ACKNOWLEDGE THE MIRACLES..2
ADVENTURE OF CREATION...3
A FUN AND EASY LIFE..4
A HOLIDAY FROM THE EVERYDAY......................................5
ALLOW YOUR RESISTANCE...6
ARE YOU FIGHTING FOR WHAT YOU WANT?......................7
ARE YOU TRYING TO FIGURE IT OUT?...............................8
ARE YOU TRYING TO MAKE YOUR LIFE HARD?..................9
ASK FOR MIRACLES...10
BE COURAGEOUS..11
BE HUMBLE..12
BEING THE BEST YOU..13
BE JOY, NOT DO TO GET JOY..14
BE STRONG..15
BE THE CHANGE..16
BE THE FAMILY YOU WISH YOU HAD................................17
BETTER OR WORSE THAN..18
BE UNFAIR...19
BE WILD..20

BLESS IT	21
BOLDLY BE YOU	22
BREAK FREE	23
BRILLIANT IDEAS	24
BRING YOU INTO THE MIX	25
CAUTIOUS	26
CELEBRATE	27
CHALLENGE YOURSELF	28
CHANGE	29
CHANGE, NOT FIX	30
CHILDLIKE	31
CHOICE OVER POSSESSIONS	32
CHOOSE HAPPINESS NOW	33
CHOOSE SOMETHING ELSE	34
CLEAR AND SPACIOUS	35
COMPASSION	36
COMPETITION	37
CONSTRUCTIVE CRITICISM	38
CONSULT WITH A YOUNGER VERSION	39
CONTRIBUTION	40
CONTROL VS LOVE	41
CREATE AND GENERATE	42
CREATE SOME SPACE	43
DEFENDING ABUSE	44
DEMAND OF YOURSELF	45
DIVINE ORDER	46

DO NOT BE AFRAID TO GIVE	47
DO NOT FEAR LOSING FRIENDS	48
DO NOT MAKE ISSUE OF YOUR ISSUE	49
DON'T WAIT TO LIVE YOUR LIFE	50
DO YOU GIVE YOURSELF ENOUGH CREDIT?	51
DREAM BIG AND RECEIVE BIG	52
EASE	53
EASY DOES IT	54
EMBRACE THE FUTURE	55
ENDINGS AND BEGINNINGS	56
ENERGY MATCHING	57
EXERCISE	58
FALSE GODS	59
FEELING SAFE	60
FEELING SORRY FOR YOURSELF	61
FIND A DIFFERENT WAY	62
FINISH WHAT YOU HAVE STARTED	63
FIRST WORLD PROBLEMS	64
FOCUSED INTENTION	65
FOCUS ON YOUR STRENGTHS	66
FORGIVE EVERYTHING FROM THE BEGINNING OF TIME	67
FREE YOUR VOICE	68
FUN IS THE NEW HARD WORK	69
GET BUSY	70
GIGGLE	71
GIVE FROM THE HEART	72

GLORY	73
GOLDEN OPPORTUNITY	74
GO OUTSIDE YOUR COMFORT ZONE	75
GRATITUDE	76
GREED	77
GRIEF	78
GROWTH	79
HAIL MARY PASS	80
HAVE MERCY	81
HONOUR YOUR BOUNDARIES	82
HONOUR YOUR TRUE FEELINGS	83
HOPE	84
HOW DIFFERENT CAN YOU BE?	85
HOW EASY CAN IT GET?	86
HOW STUPID CAN YOU BE?	87
HUMOUR	88
HURT FEELINGS	89
I'M THE BOSS OF ME	90
INCLUSION	91
INFINITE SUPPLY	92
INNER PEST	93
INNOCENCE	94
INSPIRATION IS EVERYWHERE	95
IS IT RELEVANT?	96
IT CAN HAPPEN FOR YOU	97
IT COMES DOWN TO CHOICE	98

IT DOESN'T MATTER	99
IT'S ALL FORGIVEABLE	100
IT'S NOT ABOUT YOU	101
IT'S OK TO BE WEIRD	102
IT'S TIME TO LEAVE THE UNHEALTHY SITUATION	103
IT WILL GET DONE	104
JOY	105
JOY IS A VALUABLE PRODUCT	106
JOY IS POSSIBLE AND ALLOWED	107
JUDGMENT IS A SELF-FULFILLING PROPHECY	108
KINDNESS	109
KINDNESS OF GOD/UNIVERSE	110
LEAN ON YOUR FAITH	111
LEAVE THE PAST BEHIND	112
LET YOUR GUARD DOWN	113
LIGHTEN UP	114
LIVE LIFE	115
LOOK INSIDE YOURSELF	116
LOVE	117
LOVE LIFE	118
MAKE JOKES	119
MAKE STUFF HAPPEN	120
MOODS	121
MOTHER HEALING	122
NEVER BE AFRAID TO LOSE	123
NEVER GIVE UP	124

NEW EXPERIENCES	125
NO JUDGMENT	126
NONE OF IT IS WASTED	127
NOTHING COMPARES TO YOU	128
NOTICE THE SIGNS	129
NOT YOUR CONCERN	130
OBLIGATIONS	131
OLD RUTS	132
ORIGINAL YOU	133
OUT OF YOUR HANDS	134
PATIENCE AND PERSISTENCE	135
PEOPLE SUCK. SO WHAT?	136
PERSISTENCE	137
PERSONAL GROWTH	138
PLAY	139
PRACTICE, PRACTICE, PRACTICE	140
PRAYER	141
PROPER DISTRIBUTION	142
PROSPERITY	143
PSSST YOU'RE AN ADULT NOW	144
PUNISHMENT AND REWARD	145
PURIFICATION	146
QUESTION SHOULD	147
QUIT SHOULDERING THE BURDEN	148
RECOGNIZE WHAT IS MEANINGLESS	149
RECOGNIZING DIVINE GUIDANCE AND THE IMPOSTERS	150

REFUSING IS NOT CHOOSING	151
RELAX. STUFF HAPPENS	152
RELEASE CONTROL	153
RELEASE DOUBT	154
RELEASE STRUGGLE	155
RELEASE REVENGE	156
REMOVAL OF THE SHOULDS AND HAVE TOS	157
RIGHTEOUS INDIGNATION IS A KILLER	158
SAVOURING PLEASURE	159
SELF-RESPECT	160
SENSITIVITY	161
SEXY	162
SIMPLIFYING YOUR LIFE	163
SOMETIMES OTHERS AREN'T AS KIND AS YOU	164
SPACE	165
SPEED UP	166
SPREAD THE JOY	167
START DELEGATING	168
STAY ON POINT	169
STOP BEING NORMAL	170
STOP RUSHING	171
STOP THE CYCLE	172
STOP THINKING	173
STOP ANALYZING FEAR	174
SURPLUS ENERGY	175
TENACITY AND DETERMINATION	176

THE ASK	177
THE PROBLEM WITH YOU/ME IS	178
THERE IS ALWAYS ENOUGH TIME	179
THERE IS NOTHING WRONG WITH YOU	180
THE STORY CALLED YOUR LIFE	181
TIME	182
TIME TO MOVE ON	183
TOMORROW IS YOUR LAST DAY	184
TREAT OTHERS LIKE YOU WISH TO BE TREATED, NOT HOW YOU WERE TREATED	185
TURN NECESSITY INTO PRIORITY	186
VALIDATION COMES FROM YOU	187
VICTORY!	188
VISION OF YOUR FUTURE	189
WAITING FOR SOMETHING BETTER	190
WHAT ARE YOU ROMANTICIZING?	191
WHAT ARE YOU SO AFRAID TO LOSE THAT IT CONTROLS YOU?	192
WHAT FAMILY ROLE ARE YOU PLAYING?	193
WHAT IF CHEAP CHEAPENS?	194
WHAT IS POSSIBLE HERE?	195
WHAT QUESTION ARE YOU ASKING?	196
WHAT'S YOUR GO-TO PROTECTION STANCE?	197
WHAT YOU ARE AFRAID OF IS A FALSE THREAT	198
WHEN WILL YOU BE HAPPY?	199
WHERE DO I GO FROM HERE?	200
WHO ARE YOUR ACCUSERS?	201

WHO'S NOT LOVING YOU?	202
WILL YOU ALLOW FOR THE MIRACLE?	203
WINNERS, LOSERS, AND THE ONES YOU DON'T COUNT	204
WITHIN YOU, AS YOU	205
WONDERFUL SURPRISES	206
WORTH WAITING FOR	207
WRITE DOWN YOUR THOUGHTS AND FEELINGS	208
YOU ARE A CONTRIBUTION	209
YOU ARE FEARLESS	210
YOU ARE NOT SEPARATE FROM SOURCE	211
YOU ARE OK	212
YOU ARE VALUABLE	213
YOU CAN ASK FOR ANYTHING	214
YOU CAN DO IT	215
YOU CAN GET SH!T DONE	216
YOU CAN'T FIX ANYONE	217
YOU CREATED THIS SITUATION AND YOU HAVE THE POWER TO CHANGE IT	218
YOU DON'T HAVE TO FIGURE EVERYTHING OUT	219
YOU'RE ON THE RIGHT PATH	220
YOU ROCK	221
YOUTHFUL WISDOM	222
ABOUT THE AUTHOR	223

ACKNOWLEDGEMENTS

I thank all my Facebook friends who read and enjoy these daily inspirations. Knowing that I can be of service to help brighten your day is such a joy.

A special thanks to my help from heaven – specifically my mom and my brother Gary. I can feel your encouragement to continue creating more in this life. Thank you for having my back.

I also wish to thank my children for inspiring me to inspire! You are such a blessing in my life and I don't know what I would do without you.

HOW THIS BOOK CAME INTO BEING

Since the fall of 2013, I have been writing a daily inspiration on Facebook. Every morning I sit at my computer and ask for an inspiration. Then, I write whatever comes to me.

Each day is an original gift given to me from the Universe to share with the world.

After a few years of doing this practice, several friends of mine began saying to me that I should make a book out of these daily inspirations. Each of these friends received this message independently from one another. I realized the Universe was desperately trying to get me to hear this message. I have finally decided to listen.

I published Inspirations for a Brighter Day Volume I in January of 2018. I have had such a encouraging response that I decided it was time to release Volume II.

It is my hope and intent that this book provide you with timely insight and give you just the message you need to hear when you need to hear it. May these inspirations fill your life with joy, harmony, contentment, insight, and new awareness.

If you wish to follow the latest inspirations, please go to www.facebook.com/faythompsoninspires. Each day a new inspiration is posted, hopefully, just for you.

HOW TO USE THIS BOOK

This book can be utilized in many ways. Feel free to use it in any way that inspires you for your personal use. Some suggestions are as follows:

You can read it from front to back.

You can use it as a daily meditative practice, making notes of what messages and guidance may come to you while you ponder each individual message.

You can use this book like your own personal Magic 8 Ball. Ask a question and open to a page. See what it says.

You can also ask a generic question such as, "What inspiration in this book would be most beneficial for me to pay attention to today?" Then, flip to a page and see what is there.

You can ask what page holds the message that would be most beneficial and contributive to you. Whatever number you receive, turn to that page and read.

You can flip to the Table of Contents, run your finger down the list until your finger stops. See where you are at, then go to that page.

You can also ask for what letter of the alphabet your message starts with. Go to the table of contents, which is listed alphabetically, to the letter you received, and run your finger down the list until your finger stops. That will be your message.

No matter how you use this book, have fun. Take it lightly and read with an open mind. There is no right or wrong way. Just do what is fun for you.

After reading the inspiration, you may wish to take a moment to apply what you've read. Many of the inspirations contain questions to ponder or actions to carry out. Really allow yourself to apply whatever is being suggested. Change can only happen by changing our usual habits and thought patterns. These inspirations are designed to do that, but will only yield results if you are willing to truly surrender to what is being offered. I urge you to just take a moment to see how the message applies to you and your life.

Finally, when asking yourself the questions given in these inspirations, allow the awareness to come from your heart and your knowing. Your knowing does not come from your head. You do not think when you are acting from knowing. The object is to function from awareness and your knowing – instead of thinking about it. Keep your head out of it. Always go with, "What do I know?"

P.S. – You always know everything you need to know. If

you find yourself saying, "I don't know", relax, breathe, and trust that you do know. Ask yourself, "If I did know, which I do, what would it be?" Allow the answer to come from somewhere other than your head. It will if you let it. Your knowing is always present.

P.P.S. – No matter what inspiration you receive, please never use it to judge you or others. They are meant to illuminate what choices you have been making, so that you can get a better understanding of why things are the way they are for you, and open space for you to either be just as you are or change if that is what you desire. They are not meant to judge you or your choices as right or wrong.

ACCEPT HEAVEN'S HELP

Just because you ask for help doesn't mean you take it. In fact, whenever you ask for help, it is offered and available. It is a two step process – ask and receive. This means surrendering to the fact that you don't know it all, you don't have to do it all, and that others can do things better than or just as good as you. Heaven doesn't send garbage. Therefore, when you ask for help, trust it will come and it will be divine.

NOTES:

_____

_____

_____

_____

_____

_____

_____

_____

ACKNOWLEDGE THE MIRACLES

We take time everyday to acknowledge the problems and hardships in our lives. Is it time to start acknowledging the miracles instead? Doing so will create more miracles and more joy. Today, ignore the issues and hardships and proclaim that blessings and miracles are the only things getting your attention today. You may be surprised at how much is there.

NOTES:

_____

_____

_____

_____

_____

_____

_____

_____

_____

ADVENTURE OF CREATION

You crave adventure. Create it. How often do you spend your energy on creating predictability? Or the known? The adventure is in the unknown. The adventure is in the fun of new experiences and thrill of what could be. How dull do you have to make your life for it to be predictable? Get out of predictability and choose adventure today. Try something new. Allow for something unexpected. Create without needing to know what the outcome will look like.

NOTES:

_____

_____

_____

_____

_____

_____

_____

_____

A FUN AND EASY LIFE

What comes to mind when you read that? Is it a lazy life with no substance? Or is it exciting and joyful? We seem to have the notion that a fun and easy life would mean a life without meaning, substance, or value. Perhaps it is because we, as a society, do not value fun or ease. Only we can change that. Are you willing to dare to value fun and ease in your life today? Are you willing to have a fun and easy life? What's one thing you can do today to make that happen?

NOTES:

A HOLIDAY FROM THE EVERYDAY

Do you worry about the same things everyday? Do you wonder how to fix a situation or feel powerless on how to make something happen? Why not take a holiday from your everyday thinking? Why not put those worries and thoughts aside while you go on a vacation from thinking? Where would your mind go? How much better does it make you feel to go there? Give yourself the time off to do that today. Have a holiday from the everyday.

NOTES:

_____

_____

_____

_____

_____

_____

_____

_____

_____

ALLOW YOUR RESISTANCE

Resistance to your resistance only causes more resistance. Sit quietly and allow all the resistance you are aware of to be. Do not resist it. Just let it be. What do you notice? You may find you no longer fight it. This means you come out of resistance and into receiving - which is immensely relieving. Allow for your resistance today, without resistance to it, and see what happens.

NOTES:

ARE YOU FIGHTING FOR WHAT YOU WANT?

There is a difference between going for what you want and fighting for what you want. Going for it means you are doing it, no matter what. You're on your way and nothing can stop you. Fighting for it means you are battling obstacles and enemies. It's a fight, often to the death. Would you be willing to stop fighting and just go for it? You can if you're willing.

NOTES:

___

___

___

___

___

___

___

___

___

ARE YOU TRYING TO FIGURE IT OUT?

Trying to figure it out is a life sentence to be attached to your problem. When you try to figure things out, you are being the energy of not knowing (which is why you need to figure it out), and the energy of someone who has a problem. The Universe matches your energy exactly to create your life. Therefore, when trying to figure it out, the Universe can only give you more of the problem, so that you can continue to try to figure it out. Instead, be the energy of "This is changing." or "I'm done with this." Then, the Universe has no option but to change it or be done with it.

NOTES:

_____

_____

_____

_____

_____

_____

_____

ARE YOU TRYING TO MAKE YOUR LIFE HARD?

In this reality, we are taught that somehow a hard life is a noble one. How much do you have to judge yourself for not having as hard of life as everyone else seems to be able to have? Would you be willing to forego all this nonsense and allow your life to soften? Would you allow yourself the soft and cushy life you desire but have been taught to hate and judge? What if life was soft and cushy? It's kind of wonderful. Allow for it and dissolve all the lies that tell you that the soft and cushy life is wrong, wimpy, weak, and not noble. It takes great strength and character to soften. It's a very noble act.

NOTES:

_____

_____

_____

_____

_____

_____

_____

ASK FOR MIRACLES

How often do we struggle, just get by, or go through hardship in a day? What if we stopped that and started asking for miracles? What if we started asking, "What would it take to have or create a miracle here?" Focus on struggle. Get struggle. Focus on miracles. Get miracles. Where's your focus?

NOTES:

_____

_____

_____

_____

_____

_____

_____

_____

_____

BE COURAGEOUS

Face your problems head on with confidence and courage and you will emerge victorious. Know that no energy is stronger than your ability to choose something different. You are capable of moving out of any situation and towards any situation with grace and ease. Ask for that ability to be awakened and strengthened within you. When you refuse to be a helpless victim, you begin to find newfound strength and confidence to go in a different direction and change. Tackle things head on today, and know you have the full power of the Universe supporting you with every step.

NOTES:

_____

_____

_____

_____

_____

_____

_____

_____

BE HUMBLE

Know that all things come to you come from the grace and abundance of the infinite Universe, which we are all part of. No one is greater than us. No one is lesser than. You never need worry you are not enough. Please do not put yourself under another. It does not become you. Do not feel the need to be better than. It creates too much stress to need to achieve status. Let all glory go to the magic of creation and know all that you ask for shall come to you.

NOTES:

BEING THE BEST YOU

When you try to be the best, you must look to every other person who could best you as competition. It always leads you to focus on others' choices - never your own. When you decide to be the best you, there is no competition. There is no looking outward. There's only you working with you, listening to you, cheering you on, and becoming better everyday.

NOTES:

BE JOY, NOT DO TO GET JOY

Be joy today. People often go straight to doing things that they think will bring them joy. The former provides immediate results. The latter creates frustration, struggle, and hard work for little reward. Be joy. Doing doesn't create being. Being, on the other hand, inspires you to do things that creates results. Pay attention to what joy you can be today and you will find that everything you do will be a joyful experience.

NOTES:

_____

_____

_____

_____

_____

_____

_____

_____

BE STRONG

You are stronger than you think. You have the power to succeed and overcome any obstacle in your path. Use your strength wisely by being strong in your faith in yourself, in others, and in the Universe, instead of trying to stronghold the situation and using your strength to control people or the situation - which will weaken you. You are a force to be reckoned with. Remember that force is made of love, truth, and conviction that anything is possible. When you let that be your strength, a greater outcome is inevitable and assured.

NOTES:

_____

_____

_____

_____

_____

_____

_____

_____

_____

BE THE CHANGE

We must be the change in order to have the change. If you be the one who wishes things would change, then you will only create more things that you wish would change. If you desire peace in the world, you must be at peace in your world, no matter what is going on. If you desire a new car, then you must be the energy of having a new car and not someone who keeps complaining about what they wished they had. This principle applies across the board. Go. Be the change and the change will be.

NOTES:

BE THE FAMILY YOU WISH YOU HAD

You are unique and amazing in your own way. Sometimes it may seem that in order to belong to your family, that you have to be like them. Family is not about being like your parents or siblings. It is to support you in being you, and you are there to support them in being them. How do you do that? Lead by example. Be the family member you wish you had. Be different. Be the black sheep, the odd duck, and the one who doesn't fit. Show that it is ok to be your own person and that no matter what, you will honour who you are. Why you? Because maybe, you came to make a difference. Maybe you came to show them a new way.

NOTES:

_____

_____

_____

_____

_____

_____

_____

_____

BETTER OR WORSE THAN

How many of us make us better or worse than someone or something else? In the making of us better or worse, we exclude ourselves from the group. We become, by our very own hand, an outcast. The Universe includes everything. Infinity includes everything. Would you be willing to include you in infinity? Or are you better or worse than that?

NOTES:

BE UNFAIR

Playing by the rules and making the playing ground fair, you hold yourself and the world back from your greatness. When a sports team has a star player that can outplay the rest, is it fair? You are the star player of your life. Will you be that? Will you be the one that is so amazing that it inspires and pushes people to bring out their best? Or will you be fair by bringing yourself down to the lowest common denominator? What contribution does that make to the world? NONE. How much more successful could you be if you really brought you to the game? Be unfair today. Be you because nothing can compare.

NOTES:

BE WILD

Take the controls off today and go hog wild. What if you were wild with joy? What if you were wild with ideas… with possibility… with choice? We have spent too much of our lives believing we must be contained. Containment only leads to feeling trapped. Be wild today. Release the chains and the controls. Let go of the conformity and no longer follow the masses. Stick out. Stand out. And let yourself be.

NOTES:

BLESS IT

Whatever it is, bless it. When we judge something as wrong, we curse it. When we curse, we damn and condemn. If we bless it, we create a blessing. Whether it be an annoyance, a pet peeve, an upset, or the very existence of something you wish didn't exist - bless it. Bless you and your existence as well. Only beautiful things can come out of blessings because it is a beautiful act. Only ugly things can come out of cursing because it is an ugly act. No matter what it is, bless it.

NOTES:

_____

_____

_____

_____

_____

_____

_____

_____

BOLDLY BE YOU

We often shrink to other's ideas of how we should be. What if you boldly allowed yourself to be you? Let go of the worry that the world will be pissed off at you for boldly being you. When you do, you'll realize the world is not pissed off at you. Those people are pissed off at themselves for not being them. This gives them a chance to make a different choice. It gives them a chance to be themselves.

NOTES:

_____

_____

_____

_____

_____

_____

_____

_____

BREAK FREE

Break free of your routine today and try doing something different. Often we don't want to be wrong or make a mistake, so we just stop trying new things altogether. Break free of this. Allow yourself to look silly, make a blunder, and laugh at yourself. It is so freeing. Break out of the lines drawn out for you that confine and control you. Go past those lines and into new experiences and breathe in the fresh air that comes with that. No more same old same old. Time for NEW NEW NEW!!!!

NOTES:

BRILLIANT IDEAS

Whenever you get ideas that give you excitement, a thrill, or tingles it is divine guidance speaking through you. Act upon them. Do not let the voices of doubt, disappointment, and fear stop you from moving forward. Keep asking what your next step is and it will come to you. You are full of brilliant ideas. Now is the time to allow yourself to experience how brilliant they really are. Put fear aside and act upon them… now!

NOTES:

BRING YOU INTO THE MIX

No matter what task you are doing, if you bring you into the mix you will enjoy yourself. Why? Because you actually enjoy your own company. You love it when you are present. You love it when you are involved in what you are doing. Sometimes we back away, go through the motions, and try to be as far away as possible from what we are doing. That is never fun. So show up! Bring you into the mix and notice how much better everything becomes.

NOTES:

_____

_____

_____

_____

_____

_____

_____

_____

CAUTIOUS

Being cautious is like saying there is something to fear; there is something out there that could hurt me so I had better be cautious and hold myself back. Would you be willing to dump being cautious for being aware? When you are fully aware, you fear nothing. You don't draw back out of fear or in case something bad happens. When you are aware, you know immediately if you should leave a situation or change course. You are always making sound decisions when you are aware. You are not making decisions when you are cautious.

NOTES:

CELEBRATE

Celebrate today. What do you celebrate? Does it matter? By merely deciding to celebrate, you immediately realize that anything and everything can be celebrated, and life becomes instantly more fun. Oh yay, my toothpaste tastes good. Oh joy, I have clean clothes. Oh bliss, I received my water bill today. See, it doesn't matter what you celebrate. It just matters that you do celebrate. Joy comes out of celebration. Life's a party. Make it fun.

NOTES:

_____

_____

_____

_____

_____

_____

_____

_____

_____

CHALLENGE YOURSELF

Go outside your comfort zone and push yourself past your perceived limits. When you do, you may find you are limitless. There is no boundary to what you are capable of except for the boundary you put in place. When you decide to pass that boundary, you will find that it wasn't really real. If it was, you wouldn't be able to surpass it. Challenge yourself to break outside the lines today. They aren't really real anyway.

NOTES:

CHANGE

Invite change into your life. For some reason, we resist change while simultaneously wishing for things to be different...better...which can only occur with change. Allow for change today. Invite it in. If you think something can't change, then change your mind about that. You may find that is all the change that is required.

NOTES:

_____

_____

_____

_____

_____

_____

_____

_____

_____

_____

CHANGE, NOT FIX

What if we stopped trying to fix what we are judging as wrong, and instead chose to change entirely? Fixing means having a slightly better version of the same old crap. Change means something new is possible that's not crappy at all. What if fixation on fixing is causing the hardships in your life? What if fixing is what keeps you focused on problems instead of creating solutions? What have you been trying to fix that simply requires changing? Hmmm...

NOTES:

CHILDLIKE

Try approaching your day from a child's eyes. Be childlike today. Look at situations with curiosity and wonder, joy and delight. What might change for you if you lost your aging, adult eyes and perspective? You may find life doesn't have to be so rigid or hard. Allow yourself to be 7 today - 10 max - and see what happens!

NOTES:

CHOICE OVER POSSESSIONS

Who or what owns you? Are you willing to take back your ability to choose and no longer be owned by the people and things in your life? Are you willing to be a choice instead of a possession? When you release yourself from having no choice but to follow the dictates of other people and things, you will feel the space and freedom to choose for you. Choose to no longer be enslaved by someone or something. Choose to have choice. Choose to have your life on your own terms.

NOTES:

_____

_____

_____

_____

_____

_____

_____

_____

CHOOSE HAPPINESS NOW

Are you choosing happiness now or are you brooding with plans to be happy in the future? Happiness can't come in the future unless you choose it now. Whatever you are fighting, forgive it; whatever you are punishing, pardon it; and whatever you are trying to gain, let go. Choose happy by releasing fight, struggle, judgment, justice, revenge, hate, guilt, proof of being right, and anything else that creates unhappiness. It is a lie that these things will give you happiness. They only give you grief. Want happiness? Be happiness. Dump everything that doesn't allow for that.

NOTES:

_____

_____

_____

_____

_____

_____

_____

_____

CHOOSE SOMETHING ELSE

Wherever you feel stuck, choose something else. We tend to believe the framework we're in is unchangeable, so we work within its parameters, never free of it, always stuck with it. You can choose to jump out of the framework. What is the underlying framework you're working from? Is it that people are mean so you attract mean people into your life to prove you are right? Is it that you are hated? So you find yourself doing annoying things that people hate? Is it that you are sick? Is it that you are pathetic? Or incompetent? Or not smart enough? Or not pretty enough? These are all lies, but if we live from the framework of them being truth we are stuck with them. Choose something else – something better, greater, grander, and different.

NOTES:

_____

_____

_____

_____

_____

_____

CLEAR AND SPACIOUS

Relax. Become aware of the loving support the entire Universe has for you by allowing your energy to expand as wide as you can - as wide as the Earth and beyond, and receive the space it is offering. This clears your energy of anything nasty or non-beneficial. When you make your energy as big as space and as infinite as possible, nothing can stick in it. Be big and expanded today and you shall clear yourself and feel great!

NOTES:

_____

_____

_____

_____

_____

_____

_____

_____

COMPASSION

Soften your heart and find allowance and kindness for all - especially for those who do not exhibit allowance and kindness. Also, have compassion for yourself. Beating yourself up or hurling insults at yourself does not make you a better person, nor does it motivate you to become your best. Try telling yourself how awesome you are instead, and mean it. Tell yourself, "I ROCK because I AM AWESOME!!!" Yeah. Then, send that sentiment out to the ones you love. Your sincere appreciation of them will bring out sincere appreciation of you. Why? Because you rock!!!!!

NOTES:

_____

_____

_____

_____

_____

_____

_____

COMPETITION

You believe in lack when you buy into competition as real. In a competitive world, there is only so much to go around, and that there can only be one winner. This is only possible in a finite universe. Remember, the Universe is infinite. Go for what you desire and do not worry that it is taking away from someone else - because it is not. Also, be happy for those who are succeeding. They are not taking away from you. They are showing you the way to be in order to have what you desire.

NOTES:

_____

_____

_____

_____

_____

_____

_____

_____

CONSTRUCTIVE CRITICISM

There is no such thing as constructive criticism. Telling someone that they have to improve is like saying, "You're not enough; you suck, and you need to change." It's actually a cruel practice. Pointing out someone's shortcomings will never make them want to change. It will only make them judge themselves and be annoyed with you. Instead, point out people's strong points. Point out that you believe in them. Point out that you know they are capable of whatever it is you wish them to do - and they will be motivated to do it. Empowerment never tells someone what's wrong with them. It always builds a person up.

NOTES:

CONSULT WITH A YOUNGER VERSION

When in doubt, go to a younger version of yourself and ask what you would have done. In the past, if you didn't get good results with what you are asking, do the opposite of what you would have done. If you were great at what you were asking, then go ahead and do what your younger self was successful at. It's just a fun, effective way to view your situation from a different point in time, which will open you up to new perspectives and insights.

NOTES:

CONTRIBUTION

How can you be a contribution to you and those around you? Usually people will do one or the other - either be a contribution to themselves which leaves out everyone else or they are a contribution to others leaving themselves out of the equation. What would be the combination of both? This way you contribute to others, and you contribute to you. Win Win.

NOTES:

_____

_____

_____

_____

_____

_____

_____

_____

_____

_____

CONTROL VS LOVE

In relationship, we often make certain demands of our partner. Denying someone choice will make them want to be free from your control. They will want to get their choice back. If you insist that they be faithful to you, for example, and exercise forced control upon them with regards to the subject, you will actually force them to take back the choice you don't want them to make. When you are grateful for someone's choice to be in your life, you offer freedom and appreciation for that person that makes them want to be around you. Release control for gratitude and appreciation - which is the true love.within you. Stop looking for it in other people. It's not there.

NOTES:

_____

_____

_____

_____

_____

_____

_____

CREATE AND GENERATE

Spend some time in the energy of creation and generation today. It doesn't matter if you create or generate anything. It doesn't matter what you create or generate. When you are in the energy of creation and generation you will create more for and in your life, instead of being in the energy of destruction and maintaining the status quo. What if you asked your money how it can create and generate more of itself? What if you asked your relationships how they can create and generate more happiness, respect, and kindness? What if you asked your business or job how it could create and generate more fun for you? Hmmm. There is no ending to the possibilities of the asking. Why aren't we asking? Ask today how to create and generate more greatness in your life, and just see where it takes you.

NOTES:

_____

_____

_____

_____

_____

_____

CREATE SOME SPACE

Create some space around you energetically and you will feel like you have room to breathe, that you have more options available to you, and that you are no longer pressured by expectation and responsibility. Take note of where the edges of your energy are right now. Are they fairly close to your body? Expand out, even farther than that, and expand your space past the edges of the Earth and beyond the edges of the Universe. Keep yourself expanded for a few moments and notice how you must relax in order to do so. Create and take up space today. In that you will find all that you need and a whole lot of room to grow.

NOTES:

DEFENDING ABUSE

Whenever we justify the abuse we receive or give, we are defending the abuse. What if it didn't need a defense or an offence? What if you can just admit it is abuse without needing to punish it or someone else? What if you could just say, "Hey, that's abuse. I'm stopping it now," without inflicting embarrassment, guilt, pity, revenge, or punishment with it. This is letting go of abuse. Fighting it is defending it. Justifying it is defending it. In order to defend, you must hang on.

NOTES:

DEMAND OF YOURSELF

Stop wanting and start demanding. No more maybes. No more "if it's no trouble" or "when you get around to it" or "maybe someday". If it is to happen, then you must demand it - of yourself and of the Universe. No excuses. No waiting. No apologies. No guilt. Just own it. Claim it. Be it. Demand it.

NOTES:

DIVINE ORDER

Everything is working in divine order. If it doesn't seem that way to you, ask "What would it take for me to believe this is working out for me?" Remove all your judgments, conclusions, and expectations of how and when something is to occur. Just know it can and will when the time is right. All is working perfectly. Get out of the way and enjoy the joy and ease of it all. If you won't, how is it supposed to come easily?

NOTES:

DO NOT BE AFRAID TO GIVE

When you give to someone it is an act of bravery. You do not know whether your gift will be received or rejected. We must remember that if you are rejected it does not have to do with you. It has to do with the other person. Perhaps they are afraid or proud or upset with something else. Be brave. Give, because we need to be there for each other. We need to be willing to give and be kind to one another, even if the person on the other end cannot be kind back right now.

NOTES:

_____

_____

_____

_____

_____

_____

_____

_____

DO NOT FEAR LOSING FRIENDS

Often we become worried that when we decide to change or become more of ourselves that we will lose friends. The true definition of a friend is someone who lets you be you, someone who will always have your back no matter what, and who will not judge you. If your "friends" don't like your choices or are willing to dump you for being or doing what you like, are they really friends? You may be better off without "friends" like that. True friends are there no matter what.

NOTES:

DO NOT MAKE ISSUE OF YOUR ISSUE

When you make something an issue, you are creating an obstacle for you to get over. Your issues are your excuses, your challenges, and your reasons why it's too hard, or impossible, or not worth trying. When you decide no issue is going to stop you, then all issues fall away because all energy goes to your target and your success. Do not make issue of your issue. It will only create issues for you.

NOTES:

DON'T WAIT TO LIVE YOUR LIFE

Live your life now. Do the things you wish to do someday now. Wishing for someday is not living and it is not creating. Take an active role in your life and take action to live it with joy and abandon. Stop waiting for the perfect moment or conditions to arise. They will arise when you commit to the thing you wish to create or experience. Decide, commit, and live!

NOTES:

DO YOU GIVE YOURSELF ENOUGH CREDIT?

How often do we give credit to someone else and leave ourselves short? What if you just allowed yourself the recognition you've been seeking? What if you acknowledged the true contribution you bring and have brought to all the wondrous things in your life? Question: What percentage of your contribution do you ignore? What percentage of credit do you give away to those it has nothing to do with? Let's ask that the percentage be zero. What would it be like if you actually gave yourself credit where credit is due?

NOTES:

_____

_____

_____

_____

_____

_____

_____

_____

DREAM BIG AND RECEIVE BIG

Let go of small thoughts and ideas. What do you really, really desire? Dream big and see yourself succeeding. Ask the Universe what needs to happen in order for what you want to appear. Then let the Universe bring the answer to you. Don't answer the question for the Universe. Get your ideas of what can't possibly happen out of the way and let yourself be guided to the possibilities of success. Dream big and know if it would bring joy to your heart, the Universe is eager to conspire with you to make it happen. Dream big and receive big. It can happen if you let it. Let it.

NOTES:

_____

_____

_____

_____

_____

_____

_____

EASE

How easy do you allow your life to be? What would you have to do or be that's different from you are currently doing or being in order to have ease in your life? What might you have to let go of to lighten and ease up your load? How easy can you make your life? Are you willing to have that change? Because you can. Stop asking how and just keep in the energy of "This is easy."

NOTES:

_____

_____

_____

_____

_____

_____

_____

_____

_____

_____

EASY DOES IT

It is time to detach, retreat, and let go so that healing can occur. Take it easy and step back. Trying to stronghold the situation only thwarts your progress. Back off and allow the forces of heaven to intervene on your behalf. All you need to do is ask. Here's a hint: When asking for help, it is best to allow yourself to relax and be helped. Micromanaging doesn't make anyone happy. So easy does it. Back away, relax, breathe, and let the flow of life show you the way. You will be happy that you did.

NOTES:

EMBRACE THE FUTURE

Are you excited about where you are headed? Do you know that tomorrow holds the promise of great things? Anything is possible and you can keep growing and thriving. Will you see your future that way? Or do you project your past into the future and worry about the same old things? There's no need for that. See a bright tomorrow. That will make you content and happy with today.

NOTES:

ENDINGS AND BEGINNINGS

The old must be released so that the new may enter. You have been asking for change. You have been wanting things to get better. In order for this to happen, the old must go, so let it. Make a space for the new improvement to come in and welcome it with open arms. If you continue to feel resentful of what was then you can never have what could be. Soften your heart, smile, and know the past is in the past. Look forward to the shiny lit path ahead and take a step toward it. No more do you have to feel victimized or hurt or wrong or helpless. Help is right in front of you. Take the angels by the hand and walk forward with relief and love in your heart. The old is over. Let the new begin.

NOTES:

_____

_____

_____

_____

_____

_____

_____

ENERGY MATCHING

Whatever energy you emit is what will be created for you. If have been desiring something and doing visualization, prayer, affirmation, and positive thinking without result, then it is because you are not matching your energy to the thing that you wish to come to fruition. Allow yourself to become an energy match to the thing you desire. Let your guards down and lighten up. Come into a state of gratitude. Allow for it to be without need for you to be something other than you are. When you match the energy, let it go. And that is all that is needed.

NOTES:

EXERCISE

It is time to get up and move that body! Are you feeling sluggish? Move! Are you lacking energy? Move! When you move your body it gets stuck, sluggish energy to flow. Don't buy into the lie that lying down and being still will give you energy. Unless there is a logical, good reason for you to be tired (such as you lifted heavy objects for a day or were awake for 24 hours straight), you do not need rest. You need movement. So get up, get going, and get moving! Then feel how much better you feel.

NOTES:

_____

_____

_____

_____

_____

_____

_____

_____

FALSE GODS

Anything or anyone that you have given power over you, authority, or mad superior to you is a false god. Similarly, you have made yourself a false god if you are controlling someone, believe you have authority over someone, or are superior to someone. False gods are false - not true or real. When we release our belief in them to have any say in our lives, their power falls away. When we put our faith back into the true Source, whether you call that God, the Universe, Consciousness or something else, then we realize that we shall never be condemned, judged, punished, or threatened. We are in complete grace, power, and kindness. Release your false gods today and surrender to the truth. You are innocent.

NOTES:

_____

_____

_____

_____

_____

_____

FEELING SAFE

You wish to feel safe before you make a decision. Instead, make a decision and follow the safe feeling you get by being guided to something new. Do not confuse your dysfunctional comfort zone as safety. It is just what you know. To know and experience something different, you must leave comfort, make a decision, and follow the uncomfortable safe feeling of guidance.

NOTES:

FEELING SORRY FOR YOURSELF

Are you feeling sorry for yourself? If so, then recognize what you are doing. Let yourself be the pity party and acknowledge it. Then ask, "Is this what I desire for my life?" "How can this be different? Can I change?" When you go into question, you will pull yourself out of the funk you are in OR you will recognize you are choosing to stay where you are. Key point: "you are choosing". (Hint: You are always choosing.)

NOTES:

_____

_____

_____

_____

_____

_____

_____

_____

_____

FIND A DIFFERENT WAY

When you find yourself in the same situations, before you react, stop and ask "What can I do or be differently that will create the change I am seeking?" We will often be on auto-response to certain situations and that just gives us the same old crappy result. The kids are fighting so you yell at them to stop and they don't stop. Auto-response. Find a different way. Ask a question. What would it take? The people at work annoy you in the same way and you react with judgment and frustration. Auto-response. Find a different way. Ask a question. What would it take?

NOTES:

_____

_____

_____

_____

_____

_____

_____

FINISH WHAT YOU HAVE STARTED

It is time to tie up loose ends. Complete what you have started and you will feel a satisfaction and a relief you are currently missing. What is it in your life that you have been ignoring? Is there a household fix up that needs completion? Is there a relationship that needs attention or a final severing (depending on the situation)? Whatever it is, finish it. It is time.

NOTES:

_____

_____

_____

_____

_____

_____

_____

_____

_____

FIRST WORLD PROBLEMS

First world problems are actually blessings because it means you have so much that you actually have something to lose or fix or worry about. Whatever it is that stresses you, let it go and know you are truly blessed. Be in gratitude for all that is in your life and know all is continually getting better.

NOTES:

_____

_____

_____

_____

_____

_____

_____

_____

_____

_____

FOCUSED INTENTION

Keep your unwavering thoughts, feelings, and actions focused directly on your target, and you will make your mark. The first question to ask yourself is, "Do I have a target? Do I know where I'm going and what I want?" When you know where you're going it is much easier to get there! So decide what you want and take action with your focused intention to get there. Focus. Focus. Focus and let nothing distract you from your mission.

NOTES:

_____

_____

_____

_____

_____

_____

_____

_____

_____

FOCUS ON YOUR STRENGTHS

You have so much to offer with your own unique signature. It doesn't make sense to spend time berating yourself for the things that are not your strong suit. What are you good at? What is something that comes easy to you? What is going well in your life? Focus upon that and feel grateful for what comes naturally to you. It's part of your grace. If you aren't good at something and have no desire to be good at it, don't focus upon it. Leave it for others. If you can't, then do the best you can celebrating how you are improving and learning.

NOTES:

FORGIVE EVERYTHING FROM THE BEGINNING OF TIME

You are an infinite and eternal being. This is not your first crack at living. It is time for us to forgive everything from the beginning. Forgive the wars, the torture, all who were involved in the crucifixion, the Crusaders, the Inquisition, and the things we don't even know about. It's time to forgive yourself for any contribution in it all and to forgive all those you perceive as causing those things. This is really forgiving the past - the whole past - which you are a part of. This will bring a new slate moving forward and free you from things you don't even realize are holding you down.

NOTES:

FREE YOUR VOICE

Ever feel like no one hears you? Does it ever seem like nobody's listening? Do you realize that nobody includes you? Saying nobody is listening creates nobody listening. Stop worrying about others and start listening to your own voice. If it didn't have to say the right thing or the thing that others want to hear, what would it really like to say? What does it really desire for you to hear? Free your voice from nobody listening, by letting it know you are.

NOTES:

FUN IS THE NEW HARD WORK

Fun has always created better results than hard work. This doesn't mean you goof off and do nothing. It means you goofily create - with joy, silliness, and wonder. Whatever you are doing, when you add fun to it, it will get done faster and better. Hard work basically means it's hard - so you have to struggle, get upset, be stressed, and possibly loathe what you are doing. Fun means it's intriguing, you can laugh, be curious, and possibly truly love what you are doing. Fun is the new hard work. Remember that today. What if everywhere you are working hard became fun?

NOTES:

_____

_____

_____

_____

_____

_____

_____

_____

GET BUSY

Get busy as a bee! It is time to start taking action towards your goal. As you do, with a happy heart, you are ensured sweet victory! Go ahead. You can do it. Just take the first step and the next foot will follow. As you fly from flower to flower you will see you have all the resources you need to make your honey a reality. So, get on with it. Your life is created by you. It is time to get involved and make it your own. And don't forget to stop and smell the roses as you go about your business. It makes the journey that much more enjoyable!

NOTES:

GIGGLE

Laughter is the most healing energy on the planet yet everyone seems to find reasons not to laugh. Laugh, giggle, enjoy, and be merry no matter what! Do not wait for things to be the way you wish before you do. Just do it and then things might have a chance in becoming what you wish. Every time you think "this is not a laughing matter" is the exact place where a giggle should be placed. Giggle and heal the world. Lord knows we have tried the opposite for centuries and it hasn't gotten us anywhere. So LOL - HaHaHa - insert funny face here - joke there - giggle inappropriately - just laugh.

NOTES:

GIVE FROM THE HEART

How often do we give from our head? "Oh, they need that. I'm going to help them." This can often be felt and seen as controlling and judgmental with a resistance that answers back - "Don't tell me what I need." When we give from the heart, it happens easily, is received graciously, and truly you as the giver are just as touched as the one you give to. Giving from the heart requires you to give with a vulnerability that allows you to be open. It's done as a kindness, not as charity. You will always know when it comes from the heart because the appreciation will be felt. Who are trying to help from your head? Go to your heart instead.

NOTES:

_____

_____

_____

_____

_____

_____

_____

GLORY

When you seek glory for yourself, it alludes you. When you end up fighting to prove how glorious you are, you end up looking like a fool or a braggart. When you realize that you have glory within from being connected to the infinite Universe and nothing is separate from you, you will never feel lost, never need to prove, and never be left without again. Release yourself from having to prove yourself. When you stop, you will feel the true glory of being you.

NOTES:

_____

_____

_____

_____

_____

_____

_____

_____

GOLDEN OPPORTUNITY

Doors are opening for you right now. Walk through them! Don't delay or ponder, "Is this a good idea?" If it feels right, don't over-think it. Just go! There are wonderful things in the works for you, but you still must say yes to life and allow yourself to receive. Don't let your fear hold you back. Imagine there is a golden door in front of you that emanates white light. Notice how it opens to you. Walk through it. Allow yourself to leave all else behind knowing anything you require will be waiting for you on the other side. Go and don't look back. Congratulations. You have just told the Universe you accept the golden opportunity it is presenting to you. Be thankful and forget about it until you are inspired to act.

NOTES:

_____

_____

_____

_____

_____

_____

_____

GO OUTSIDE YOUR COMFORT ZONE

Do you want change or do you want comfort? Comfort is what you already know and are familiar with which essentially means same old same old. Change is something different, something not familiar, and therefore, initially, uncomfortable until you get comfortable with the unfamiliar and then it becomes familiar. Change requires some discomfort – but it is temporary. Are you willing to have the courage to widen your comfort zone for the change you wish?

NOTES:

___

___

___

___

___

___

___

___

___

GRATITUDE

Pay attention to what you are grateful for and it will bring you more. Stay stuck in the vibration of what you don't have and you will never have it. Sometimes it is difficult and it takes will power and choice to find gratitude through the sea of lack-filled thoughts floating in the air, but it is necessary and the most important work you will ever do, because the rewards are immediate and expansive. When you are gracious, life is gracious with you.

NOTES:

GREED

We think if we have too much we are being greedy. That is not greed. Greed is the act of not giving when you can give. Greed is a withholding energy. How much greed do you instill upon yourself so that you it feels like you don't have anything to give? How much do you withhold from yourself, thinking you are not being greedy but really are only denying yourself? If you are withholding, then that's greedy energy, because you are not allowing the full contribution of you to come through. Receive more. Withhold less.

NOTES:

_____

_____

_____

_____

_____

_____

_____

_____

_____

GRIEF

Grief occurs with a feeling of loss. When we realize we carry the love and memories with us in our hearts and open our hearts to acknowledge that, it lessens the grief. Opening the heart is an act of vulnerability. It can be scary to do, but the pay off is worth it. So allow your heart to open and acknowledge what you have, have always had, and will always have in times of grief. I'm not saying it will be easy, but it will bring ease.

NOTES:

GROWTH

Growth requires change. A flower can't stay a seedling and expect to bloom. A toddler can't stay the same and expect to reach full height. An adult can't stay the same and expect to reach full potential. We must be willing to move forward, change, grow, get uncomfortable, and move into the unknown. Where have you stopped growing? Is it time to allow for the bloom?

NOTES:

_____

_____

_____

_____

_____

_____

_____

_____

HAIL MARY PASS

In football the Hail Mary is an attempt to throw the long pass for the touchdown because there just isn't time for anything else. How many of us don't go for the touchdown because we are too caught up in making the perfect play? How many of us could actually make miracles happen if we threw caution to the wind and went for the long shot? What is so desirable about playing it safe when in life it is always the miracles and the "I can't believe I did it" that always creates the joy, excitement, and magic in our lives? How much joy do we throw away trying to get it perfect? Throw a Hail Mary pass. Just go for it because with life there is no 4th quarter and there is no two minute warning. Remember a touchdown is a touchdown no matter how pretty it is executed. So execute. Don't think. Just throw the ball.

NOTES:

_____

_____

_____

_____

_____

HAVE MERCY

Imagine your time has come and you have met your maker. Your soul is before God for review. You are granted the right to choose your fate. There are 2 choices: Judge you and condemn you to hell for eternity or have mercy upon you. Knowing that we are all One and that whatever is done unto one is done unto all, what do you choose? Will you have mercy on your soul? Will you open your heart to forgive all of it? You don't have to wait until the time you meet your maker to choose. You can do this now. You may have noticed you already are. You may have noticed you've been doing it all along. Why? Because, God resides within you, as you. Be a merciful God.

NOTES:

_____

_____

_____

_____

_____

_____

_____

HONOUR YOUR BOUNDARIES

Knowing yourself well enough to know what works for you, what you are willing to do, and what you want to do is beneficial. Then it is also beneficial to hold your ground when others wish to violate that or impose their demands upon you. Where are you allowing yourself to be walked on? Where are you allowing yourself to be compromised by your decisions? Choose to be kind and giving, but include yourself in that equation. Whatever is not kind and giving to you is not an act of kindness. A true act of kindness always makes you feel light. Set your boundaries today, know what they are, and honour them. Do not make yourself wrong for having them. Instead, celebrate in the honouring of yourself.

NOTES:

_____

_____

_____

_____

_____

_____

HONOUR YOUR TRUE FEELINGS

Sit quietly to distinguish your own feelings from others. You would be surprised how often humans confuse the two. We look around and notice what others are feeling and adopt them as a means to fit in. Now is the time to stop this practice and truly determine your own feelings, your own wants and desires, and your own truth. This is immensely freeing, because generally your own truth will feel much better to you than someone else's. It will lead you to solutions, to surrender, letting go, and fulfillment. Honour those feelings today and set yourself free!

NOTES:

_____

_____

_____

_____

_____

_____

_____

_____

HOPE

There is always a wonderful solution to every issue and brilliant plans for you - just keep faith and have hope. Keep the spark of light alive within you. Don't let doubt, fear, and worry darken or dampen it. There is always a way. This too shall pass. And there is light at the end of the tunnel - so keep moving toward it. Never lose sight of the light. You can even carry a torch of your own light to help you on your way. It's a choice. Choose hope. Choose light and know there is always hope.

NOTES:

HOW DIFFERENT CAN YOU BE?

You are one of a kind, so why do you spend your time trying to fit in? Whenever you are trying to do the right thing you are trying to fit in. Whenever you think you got it wrong you are trying to fit in. Is now the time to stop? Is now the time to be the difference that you are? How different can you be? How freeing and relieving might that be? What if your difference is the rightness in the world that no one else can duplicate?

NOTES:

_____

_____

_____

_____

_____

_____

_____

_____

HOW EASY CAN IT GET?

Magic happens when you allow life to be easy. The more you try to make something happen then the more you struggle. The more energy of struggle you put out to the universe the more energy to struggle is given. Stop trying. Start allowing. Start asking the question: "Hmmm. How easy can this be? How easy will I allow it to be? " Get the idea? Easy Peasy = Magic.

NOTES:

HOW STUPID CAN YOU BE?

This reality defines smart as having all the right answers. What if having all the answers is the very thing that limits you? Once you have an answer, you define the limits and boundaries that the answer lives in creating a box without other possibilities. What if not having all the answers, but only questions, was the way to endless, infinite possibilities? What if you no longer needed to try to be smart all the time? I dare you to play with this today by asking, with playfulness and no judgment, "How stupid will I allow myself to be?" Be like a child - full of questions not knowing any answers, but creating wonder and joy and magic in their world. Would you allow yourself to be that stupidly happy?

NOTES:

_____

_____

_____

_____

_____

_____

_____

HUMOUR

When you come out of judgment - meaning you no longer need to be right or point out what is wrong with a situation- you will find humour in everything. Similarly when you go looking for the humour in situations, you will come out of judgment. Being right is the number one way we block joy and happiness. So find humour in things today or let go of your judgments (where you are being right or pointing out what is wrong) and notice how humorous you find things. Life is always more fun when you are amused.

NOTES:

HURT FEELINGS

Stop hurting your feelings by trying to be what everyone else wants you to be so that you don't hurt their feelings so that they don't hurt your feelings some more. Since everyone is responsible for their own happiness, so are they responsible for their own feelings. Is it time to stop hurting you? Be responsible for you today by no longer letting anyone dictate who or how you should be or act. Today honour your own feelings and desires and choose for you no matter what other people think.

NOTES:

_____

_____

_____

_____

_____

_____

_____

_____

I'M THE BOSS OF ME

You are the boss of you unless you have designated others for that job. If you find yourself fighting to get what you want, constantly doubting your decisions, or feel like you have to give up going for what you desire then you probably have made others the boss of you. Ask for the energy or energies of all your bosses to come forward and ask them, "Who were you before you were the boss of me?" then "Who were you before that?" Ask that 3 times. Then ask, "Who will you be in the future?" Then watch them leave and ask them to take all their magnetic imprinting and baggage with them. Then reclaim you as the boss of you and see if you feel any differently.

NOTES:

_____

_____

_____

_____

_____

_____

_____

INCLUSION

Everything you hold away from yourself to protect you is actually harming you. When you include energies in your world, more energy flows and you have more available to you. Inclusion requires no effort. Inclusion is what the Universe does. It doesn't exclude anything. So be like the Universe and include what you are excluding.

NOTES:

INFINITE SUPPLY

You have access to an infinite supply. Wherever you put your focus you will draw from that supply. If you focus on worry and resentment, you will pull from that supply. If you focus on goodness, kindness, and trust, you will pull from that supply. If you focus on lack of money you will receive that. If you focus on abundance of things you will receive that. So focus on the things that make you feel good, that make you smile or giggle inside. Focus on the infinite supply of joy and laughter and prosperity in the world for it is good and it is yours for the taking.

NOTES:

INNER PEST

Your inner pest is something that nags at you and won't go away. It is only a pest because it wants something. Give it to it. Everything you have been denying and resisting to make it go away hasn't worked. So give it what it wants - probably recognition and appreciation. Once it has it, it will not pester you again.

NOTES:

INNOCENCE

The Universe has no judgment of you at all. None. Zip. Zero. Everything you think is wrong with you; everything you feel guilty for are just judgments from you, of you, or from others or of others, but they are NOT from God or the Universe. You are innocent. You are not bad or good. You just are innocence. Pure and simple. What would you be capable of receiving if you believed you deserved it? Innocence is all deserving. What could you create if you dropped the judgments of why you can't or shouldn't? Innocence is all knowing, all trusting, all you. You are innocence.

NOTES:

_____

_____

_____

_____

_____

_____

_____

INSPIRATION IS EVERYWHERE

Inspiration is everywhere. Look around. What can lift your spirits right now? Is it the sun? The sky? A child's laugh? A book? There is no limits to inspiration. Let yourself be inspired. Look outside yourself and find yourself feeling lifted by the existence of joyous creation around you. I wonder what is possible to create from that inspiration now?

NOTES:

IS IT RELEVANT?

Anything you are stressing about you may wish to ask if it is relevant. We often make things matter much more than they actually do. What are you making so important that actually isn't important at all? What have you made a higher priority than your laughter, fun, gratitude, and appreciation? If whatever you are dealing with doesn't enhance those things, then it really is time to ask, "Is this really relevant?"

NOTES:

IT CAN HAPPEN FOR YOU

In order for it to happen, you must have faith in you. You must choose for that possibility to exist for you. You must boldly believe in yourself when possibly no one else will, and you are not alone. The Universe has your back and whatever you believe, it delivers. So if you believe it can't or won't happen, the Universe grants that wish. If you believe that it can, the Universe grants that instead. So have your own back. It can happen for you.

NOTES:

_____

_____

_____

_____

_____

_____

_____

_____

IT COMES DOWN TO CHOICE

All the hoping, wishing, praying, and thinking about it will not create a life that you love. It comes down to you. It comes down to you choosing what you desire and going for it with unwavering faith in yourself. Then things really start happening. But if you think I will be happy, or rich, or successful when _____ happens, then you are not actually choosing to be happy, rich, or successful. You are choosing to be a pawn in a cruel game of life. And you will lose. It comes down to you. It comes down to your choice. What are you going to choose for yourself?

NOTES:

_____

_____

_____

_____

_____

_____

_____

IT DOESN'T MATTER

Nothing matters except to the degree you make it matter. The greater degree you make something matter, the greater the amount judgment you need to either fight for or against that thing. If we don't make things matter, then there is no need for punishment, greed, revenge, hate, war, slavery or oppression. Forgiveness would be easy. Possibility would be noticed. Kindness would prevail, because we would begin to see how our actions affect others, instead of using our actions to correct and control others. Try it for today, say "it doesn't matter" to every resistance, feeling, emotion, joy, or upset that comes your way. What happens?

NOTES:

_____

_____

_____

_____

_____

_____

_____

_____

IT'S ALL FORGIVEABLE

We harbour resentments, vengeance, and revenge, all the while deciding we are right and upholding the good in the world. Does any of this make us happy? No. Our job is not to uphold justice, but to forgive. Forgiveness is what frees us from bondage, pain, and the cruelty that justice demands. No matter what it is that you have decided is unforgivable, consider that you are mistaken. All it requires is your choice to forgive it. Do, and you free yourself. Don't, and you are stuck with your justice and all it demands forever.

NOTES:

IT'S NOT ABOUT YOU

Remember, people's reactions are about them, not you. You needn't worry about someone else's upset or judgment. You care so much about them that you would do anything, even judge and criticize yourself, in order for someone not to choose to be upset. Have you noticed that even when you do that, they still aren't happy? Recognize sometimes you care more about other people's well-being than they care about their own. Let them be upset if they choose it and carry on with what brings you joy or growth, despite their grumblings. Their grumblings are not about you.

NOTES:

_____

_____

_____

_____

_____

_____

_____

_____

IT'S OK TO BE WEIRD

It is time to put your joy first and don't let other's expectations override it. Know this: When you accept yourself for who you are, so will others. It's time to come out of the pesky closet and admit who you are to yourself with honesty and, most importantly, without apology. You are who you are, and who you are is weird and wonderful perfection!

NOTES:

IT'S TIME TO LEAVE THE UNHEALTHY SITUATION

The Universe is pretty clear with this one. You can't stay in an unhealthy situation and think it's going to get better. You've tried to make it better and it's not working. Get out. Leave. Force your hand and choose a healthy situation. It's time to take control of your life and choose situations that serve you, bring you dignity and respect, and love. Leave the rest behind. What you really need will come with you. What you don't will fall away. It's time to say goodbye to the crap in your life so that you may open the door to something beautiful.

NOTES:

_____

_____

_____

_____

_____

_____

IT WILL GET DONE

Know you will make time for what is important to you. It will get done. And, if it doesn't, it will not be the end of the world. Time will go on. And so will you.

NOTES:

_____

_____

_____

_____

_____

_____

_____

_____

_____

_____

JOY

Joy is there for you and in you because in truth you are joy in your true being. Will you let it out to play? What are you proving by suffering? How many "I suffered" badges and T-shirts have you earned? Are you ready to stop going for gold in the suffering event and allow yourself some joy? Wouldn't that be winning? Let the joy out today and see where that takes you. Lose hard in the suffering round. You may just find that it doesn't really suit you.

NOTES:

JOY IS A VALUABLE PRODUCT

We have been taught that struggle, hard work, and effort are valuable products. Are they? Or are they actually pieces of crap that erode away at your enthusiasm, happiness, and well-being? Joy is often downplayed and yet, it is the one thing that will boost an immune system, create motivation and ease, and produce a higher quality result. When you are joyful, you can spend countless hours on an activity and it will never seem like hard work. You get lost in the joy of it. What if you increased the value of joy in your life and decreased the value of struggle? What might shift?

NOTES:

_____

_____

_____

_____

_____

_____

_____

JOY IS POSSIBLE AND ALLOWED

When you are depressed, feeling down, or in a funk you not only think joy is impossible, but also perhaps not allowed. Both are false. What joy have you locked away to prove you are miserable? What joy have you locked away to prove you are a victim? Is it time to put lock to key and give yourself back the space of joy? Is it time to release the proving of how hard you have it or how much you can endure? Joy is possible. It is allowed. Will you allow it for you today? Because it is your choice whether or not to allow it. Are you ready to destroy all the reasons and conditions you create to disallow joy for you? There you go. Now don't smile. Stop it! Stop smiling now. You're smiling!? Better watch out. Someone might see that joy and think your life is easy. But you wouldn't want that, would you???? (I would.)

NOTES:

_____

_____

_____

_____

_____

_____

JUDGMENT IS A SELF-FULFILLING PROPHECY

When we judge ourselves, we end up believing those judgments, and make them self-fulfilling prophecies. If you judge that you are not doing enough, you will actually do and create less than you'd like to, so that you can continue to judge yourself as not doing enough. If you judge that you are overweight, you will continue to keep or add to that weight, so that you can keep that judgment alive. Only by coming out of judgment and deciding to change (not because what you have is wrong, but because you are demanding something different for yourself without reason or question) will your issue change. Pay attention to where you judge yourself. Then, let yourself know it isn't real or true and that when you choose to, you will have something different. That's when change will happen.

NOTES:

___

___

___

___

___

KINDNESS

Your kindness is one of the most valuable and contributive qualities you possess. Growing up we may not have had evidence of that. Cruelty and one-upmanship may have been seen to be more valued by "the cool kids" or even by your own family. Reclaim the power of your kindness and use it on you. Everywhere you were unkind to you by believing you did something to bring out the cruelty of others or were not enough to bring out their kindness, release. You do not make the choice for others to be cruel. That was their choice. It is your choice to choose kindness even in the face of cruelty. Will you be kind to you even though there has been cruelty? This truly is the most valuable act you can ever make for you and for us all.

NOTES:

_____

_____

_____

_____

_____

_____

KINDNESS OF GOD/UNIVERSE

God dwells within you, as you. Whatever you decide to be is God. So, is your God kind and merciful, or is your God judgmental and punishing? Are you ready to experience the depth of God's kindness and mercy? Are you ready to allow yourself to be that for you and others? It's within you. It's always been with you. Are you ready to choose that? Are you ready to let go of the judgments and all you have vowed to avenge in order to have that kindness and mercy? It's all up to you.

NOTES:

LEAN ON YOUR FAITH

Surrendering to your faith and letting it hold you up has deep power to it. Put your faith in possibility and miracles. Believe in the power of good things happening for you and others. Trust in the divine wisdom to change things in an instant. Faith requires a leap into the unknown. You can't tell faith how to work or what the outcome has to be. The moment you do that, you are putting faith in the ego, and it will always disappoint you. Stay strong. Have faith.

NOTES:

LEAVE THE PAST BEHIND

Leave your past behind because it only weighs you down. Who would you be if you had no past? What would you choose if you had no past? When would you choose it if you had no past? The big mistake we make is to allow the past to define us. It doesn't. What if that cup of coffee you drank yesterday has nothing to do with the fact you drank a cup of coffee today? What if you don't have to define yourself as a coffee drinker? What if you could just choose to have a cup of coffee -or not - when the moment arises? What if the number of people you've slept with doesn't define your innocence? What if the time you broke out in anger doesn't define your ability to be kind? Leave the past behind and choose from this moment whatever you like. You may find you make a different choice that creates a different result and then the definitions of you can fall away like the past.

NOTES:

_____

_____

_____

_____

_____

LET YOUR GUARD DOWN

Let down those guards that you think are protecting you from the world or protecting the world from you. They don't protect a damn thing but only serve to keep out the wonderful energy and abundance you could be receiving and the amazing magnificence of you that you could be gifting. When you allow yourself to become vulnerable and become the kindness you truly be, then even in the presence of unkindness, you will be in allowance and acceptance of life and everyone in it - including you. Let your guard down. It is worth the risk. Ironically, it is your greatest strength to allow yourself to be that vulnerable.

NOTES:

_____

_____

_____

_____

_____

_____

_____

LIGHTEN UP

Being serious only brings you down. It is a lie that you have to get serious about things in order for them to happen. When you are in a joyful, fun-filled, light mood, things seem to happen as if by magic. They happen easily. Seriousness = struggle. Seriousness = hard work. Fun = ease. Fun = fun. Which do you choose? Lighten up today about all the things you take so seriously and see what happens. You may just find that life lightens up with you.

NOTES:

LIVE LIFE

Are you living your life or is life being lived for you? Are you just going through the motions? Is each day not much different from the next? Or are you taking the bull by the horns and creating life as you wish it? Are you the sculptor creating a work of art? Which one sounds more exciting? Which one would give you joy or contentment? Live life today my friends. Don't let life live you.

NOTES:

LOOK INSIDE YOURSELF

Look inside yourself and you will find everything you need. There will be infinite prosperity, health, abundance, love, and acceptance. All you need to do is acknowledge and accept it is there and there it is! As humans, we have made the mistake of looking outside ourselves and looking at others to decide what we have, don't have, and for what is possible. Never compare yourself to others. It will give you a false sense of truth. So today, look inside. Any thing you think is missing, is not. Ask to be made aware of it and accept it when it is shown to you. You are complete and whole in everyway. Look inside. You'll see.

NOTES:

_____

_____

_____

_____

_____

_____

_____

LOVE

To unconditionally love you must love it all - the good the bad and the ugly. When we stop fighting and judging everything we view as wrong and surrender to the love inside of us, receiving it all, then there is nothing left to fight and all the crap falls away. A sense of peace and allowance ensues. Whatever is bugging you today, surrender and receive it all without a fight, then choose what works for you. Once you stop fighting you find the strength and space for something to change. LOVE don't fight. LOVE don't judge. LOVE and receive and all will be well.

NOTES:

LOVE LIFE

You can look at this message in 2 ways. First, your love life - have you been taking a significant other for granted? Have you been coasting? Is your love life non-existent? If so, then it is time to make time to rekindle relationships with kindness, gratitude, and some fun! If there isn't that romantic partner in your life, do the same with those around you. Feel the preciousness of the friendships you have and the gratitude you have for the opposite sex (or the same sex depending on your orientation). Secondly, you can view this message as a call to LOVE your LIFE! What in it is blessed? What are you grateful for? What can you do today to LOVE LIFE? Both will ignite the spark within you and provide for a day and life filled with love, romance, kindness, and joy!

NOTES:

_____

_____

_____

_____

_____

_____

MAKE JOKES

When we find humour in things, life becomes filled with laughter. Nothing is off limits and often the joke about the most sacred or serious thing will make the best joke or get the biggest laugh. So look for the humour, the fun, the joke, and the smile in all things today - especially the things that don't seem funny or you don't think you can laugh about. It will brighten your day...and probably someone else's too.

NOTES:

MAKE STUFF HAPPEN

If you want something to happen, put energy toward bringing it into being. If you wish you could see an old friend, call them up and commit to a date to see them. If you want to go on a trip, book the plane ticket, save the money, and go. If you want to learn a skill, enroll in the class and start. Make stuff happen.

NOTES:

MOODS

Moods are a choice. You can change the mood you are in by consciously choosing to change them. Often, we work on autopilot or we become the mood of the others around us. We don't have to. So if you don't like the mood you are in, you don't have to change others to change your mood. You can just choose to be different. Right now, what mood are you in? Can you change it to be happier or more grateful? If you think you can't, ask is it that you can't or won't? Recognize that others don't pick your mood, you do.

NOTES:

_____

_____

_____

_____

_____

_____

_____

_____

MOTHER HEALING

You may still have unresolved issues regarding your mother or motherhood. Forgive. Forgive. Forgive. Let go of anger, disappointment, and resentment. Yes, your mother has her faults. So do you. No need to ridicule each other for them. Just laugh and realize we're all doing the best we can in this big world and yep, sometimes we screw up or are not as loving or understanding as maybe we could be. Let it go. And know that when you nurture and be kind and understanding to yourself, you begin to mother that which was neglected. Be kind to yourself today and everyday. Be understanding. Be forgiving.

NOTES:

NEVER BE AFRAID TO LOSE

So often we cling to something, afraid to lose it in case we are left with nothing. The truth is, you are working with an infinite Universe. Often losing the thing you cling to opens you to a whole world of possibilities you didn't even realize was there for you. If you are afraid, then you are not divinely guided or inspired. You are controlled. When you take the risk to let go and lose, you win. Never let fear dictate your decisions. It's not on your side.

NOTES:

NEVER GIVE UP

Anything you truly desire is possible. Never give up on the making of your dreams come true. Sometimes it may take years. Sometimes it may take several tries. If it is truly what you desire, just keep believing in its actualization and it will come. Anytime you hear yourself say, "it's hopeless" it's not. What else is possible? What have you never considered that will get you closer to your goal? Never give up!

NOTES:

NEW EXPERIENCES

Try something new each and everyday. What might you choose? What are you refusing to experience because you have already concluded the outcome of the thing you have never actually experienced? What if you're wrong? How much do we stop ourselves in fear it won't be enjoyable? How enjoyable is that? Some of the best stories come from the adventures and risks we take - whether the outcome was enjoyable or not. So try something new today. What grand and glorious adventures are possible for you today? Will you choose them?

NOTES:

_____

_____

_____

_____

_____

_____

_____

_____

NO JUDGMENT

When you stop labeling everything as good and bad or right and wrong, you become happy and content with life and everyone in it. Where have you judged yourself that keeps you in the constant need to punish yourself? Where have you judged yourself that keeps you eternally making yourself wrong? What if nothing was wrong with you? Without judgment, nothing is. How refreshing might that be? So what if you're loud or selfish or too quiet or whatever? Who cares? If you do, then you are judging yourself. If you enjoy being whatever you say you are then go forth and be more. If you don't then change it. Life is just one big choice! Today, go with the "So what?"- No judgment plan. Just see what it does for you.

NOTES:

_____

_____

_____

_____

_____

_____

NONE OF IT IS WASTED

Every moment, every choice, and every experience is useful to you. It doesn't matter that you got that degree that you seemingly never use. It will come in handy someday. It doesn't matter that. you went through horrific circumstances. You will help others going through a similar situation someday. None of what you have been through is a mistake. None of it is something you should judge yourself for. None of it is wasted. You may not see how right now, but give it time. You have done nothing wrong.

NOTES:

___

___

___

___

___

___

___

___

NOTHING COMPARES TO YOU

Whenever you decide you are not enough, what is that compared to? When you compare yourself to an outside parameter, you can always be left short. When you realize you are a unique being with incomparable gifts, there is nothing to compare yourself to. What if, instead, you began asking, what is unique about me? What is the gift of my being me? These questions, when asked with sincerity, not sarcasm, will show you the answers.

NOTES:

_____

_____

_____

_____

_____

_____

_____

NOTICE THE SIGNS

The Universe sends you signs to let you know you are not alone, that you are on the right path, and to guide you in the best direction. Are you paying attention? Do you notice something repeatedly? It is a sign. Do you find pennies from heaven? Or feathers? You are not alone. You are watched over. Do you see repeating numbers like 111, 222, 333, 444...? They are signs that your angels are with you, there to help you. All you need to do is ask. If you need a sign, ask for one. Then pay attention. They are all around. And they are sent in love. What signs have you been getting and ignoring? It is time to notice the signs.

NOTES:

_____

_____

_____

_____

_____

_____

_____

_____

NOT YOUR CONCERN

This situation requires neither your input nor your judgment. If you must add your input into this situation, see all as they are in God's eyes – perfect, capable, loved, and magnificent. As humans, we often wish to put our energies into helping others, but sometimes our help is not necessary, beneficial, or even asked for. If something is not going the way you would like with regards to another person, see them as fully having the resources, wisdom, and connection to resolve this on their own or with the help of their own divine guidance. Your input may be hampering them from realizing their own power to do for themselves.

NOTES:

OBLIGATIONS

An obligation is where you feel have no other choice but to do the thing before you - whether you want to or not. It is time to look at where you feel obligated and challenge it, break it, and choose for you. Obligations control you. It is up to you to release yourself from them. And, also free others from where you have obligated them to you. Only then will you be able to choose from a place of integrity and freedom.

NOTES:

OLD RUTS

We get into ruts very easily. We do the same thing, think the same way, and act in the same manner to most things. This does not breed new possibilities. In order for new possibilities to be created, break out of your ruts. It won't necessarily be comfortable, because your brain that is used to the neural pathways you normally use will go, "Wait a minute! What the...? Go back to what I'm used to!!!!" Just remember your mind doesn't direct you. You direct your mind. Tell it that it is ok and you are seeking new possibilities. Then things start changing. Today, recognize some old ruts and start breaking free of them.

NOTES:

ORIGINAL YOU

Sometimes it is easy to get lost in others ideas, thoughts, or choices. We start mimicking others as if what they are thinking or doing is better than what we have to offer. When you close all the doors to the distractions of what others are doing, you can focus on being you - the original you - that is the best thing you will ever be. So do that today, and everyday. Shut out the distractions of others and go inward. What is truly you? Be that.

NOTES:

___

___

___

___

___

___

___

___

OUT OF YOUR HANDS

Sometimes we so wish for something to be a certain way we put enormous amounts of energy toward controlling an outcome through worry, micromanaging, or just plain meddling. Sometimes outcomes are out of our hands. You can't worry someone into health. You can't micromanage an artist and expect a great work of art. When we leave things to the Universe to handle with our humble request of what we truly would like to see, and believe in the people involved, greater things happen. Whatever is out of your hands, truly hand over and trust that the greatest outcome - no matter what it is - is to come.

NOTES:

_____

_____

_____

_____

_____

_____

_____

PATIENCE AND PERSISTENCE

What you are desiring or creating is worth waiting for. Have patience and keep your eye on the target. Don't give up before you hit your mark. Sometimes we don't always know why things take time or why we can't have it right now. Just know, if it's worth waiting for, then have patience and persistence. Don't give up.

NOTES:

PEOPLE SUCK. SO WHAT?

All the time people do stuff that's stupid, mean, thoughtless, judgmental, selfish...you name it...they suck. AND, all the time there are people who are kind, funny, helpful, thoughtful, loving, generous...you name it....and then they don't suck. And, all of these actions are held by all of us at one time or another. We suck and we don't. Don't get stuck on one sucky thing and make it a lifelong mission to focus upon it. Laugh at how people sometimes suck, then let it go. When you do, an un-sucky one will be right around the corner, lifting you up.

NOTES:

_____

_____

_____

_____

_____

_____

_____

PERSISTENCE

Do not give up on your hopes and dreams. Be persistent. If you come across a road block, use your will to tell the Universe, "I will not give up and that there must be a way that is easy and good for me to take. Show it to me!" Be persistent that you have happiness. Be persistent that you have health. Be persistent that all is well. And it must be. Never give up because others around you do not believe in miracles. Never give up because you are unsure of how it would be possible for what you want to be. Persist in the pursuit of your joy today. Trust that despite present circumstances, you will be victorious!

NOTES:

_____

_____

_____

_____

_____

_____

_____

_____

PERSONAL GROWTH

You are continually growing. You are never stagnant, even if it seems that way sometimes. Take a look back at the progress you have made. One year ago today, you were in a much different place. You have either come through obstacles or are going through more and, as always, will emerge on the other side of them better and more wise. Give yourself a pat on the back for continually growing, learning, and experiencing life in its many facets. Then take a moment to ask in what area would you like to have more growth. Move in that direction. You can't get it wrong and you will never be alone. The Universe is applauding your every move and supporting you every step of the way.

NOTES:

_____

_____

_____

_____

_____

_____

_____

PLAY

Do you spend your days as if life is play or do you spend it doing a job and getting things done. Nose to the grindstone. When we allow play in our lives, things still get done. In fact, they get done quicker and with more fun. Creativity is sparked and new creations and innovations are born. We open to other possibilities and opportunities. So play today and everyday. You may find there is more fun than you ever thought possible.

NOTES:

_____

_____

_____

_____

_____

_____

_____

_____

PRACTICE, PRACTICE, PRACTICE

With daily practice you will polish your skills and talents and increase your confidence. What is it that you would like to do but don't think you have the skill to? Just start and little by little you will get better and better. If you have an interest in something, then you most likely have an aptitude for it. Don't give up before you start. Know that it takes time. Everything is hard before it is easy. So go to that class or play that instrument or try that creative endeavour or whatever! Know you will get better and if it truly interests you, you will enjoy the results of your efforts.

NOTES:

PRAYER

Instead of worrying or deciding there is no happy outcome, give it over to the Universe, God, or the angels for resolution through prayer. You don't know what you don't know. You don't know the perfect solution. You don't know that there is not one. Open to the infinite possibilities available. Put aside all your answers, knowings, and judgments and be open to the possibility that there is something greater and better for you. Pray for it. Trust and have faith. Then, let it be.

NOTES:

PROPER DISTRIBUTION

Matters of our lives need to distributed to the proper authorities in order for smooth sailing. The things that you don't know how to deal with, put in hands of the Universe. This includes all the things you have been trying to handle without success. Your struggle has been noted; now hand it over It also includes the things that have to do with other people's lives, no matter how much you love them. Not your business. Surrender it. Not yours to deal with. The things that you can do and are capable of doing, get busy and do them. You can make choices and actions to further your own life and happiness. You are not helpless. And remember, when you are unsure, ask, "What's the proper distribution here? Who needs to handle this?"

NOTES:

PROSPERITY

Prosperity is cultivated with gratitude. When you are grateful, you are emanating the energy that miracles are made of. When you acknowledge what you desire is out there and you only need feel gratitude for that, it will have no choice but to come to you. So be grateful for the possibilities of prosperity being available to you today. Be grateful for the things that have already come your way. What if all your dreams came true? Be grateful for the possibility of that. There is so much to be grateful for, so why spend time on the things you aren't?

NOTES:

_____

_____

_____

_____

_____

_____

_____

_____

_____

PSSST YOU'RE AN ADULT NOW

Which means no one can tell what you should and should not do. You can go ahead all on your own without listening to anyone else's rules. You can be you without interference. You just need to stop acting like a child who needs permission to have fun or joy in their lives. You've got the power now. Use it.

NOTES:

PUNISHMENT AND REWARD

What most people don't realize is that these two go hand-in-hand. Where one is, the other will be present. Where are you rewarding yourself with punishment? Where are you punishing yourself in order to gain reward? When we release the need to either have reward or punishment, we come into being. We come to a place of just allowing ourselves to be grateful for what is there and open to receive all that there is in the abundant universe. There is no judgment. No deciphering what you do or do not deserve. Just allowance for you, your desires, and your choices.

NOTES:

PURIFICATION

It is time to purify your thoughts and body. Where are you feeding yourself judgment? Where are you telling yourself you are not enough? Where are you thinking you are wrong, a mistake, or a loser? Purify yourself from these lies. Why carry the weight of them around with you when they only weigh you down? Lift yourself up and cleanse the mind of that garbage. You are not a garbage can. You are a divine being - kind, amazing, miraculous! Believe it! If you won't, who will? Today is a day to purify your mind and find the Truth! You are AWESOME, just as you are!

NOTES:

_____

_____

_____

_____

_____

_____

_____

QUESTION SHOULD

Every time you hear yourself saying "I should" - stop and question it. Why should you? Because it's expected? How inspired is that? Should is not divine guidance. It is not a road to happiness. It is a road to enslavement or to being corralled into a sheep pen with all the other sheep. No more should. Instead, what is light and joyful or inspired? I can guarantee most of the time that will not be what others think you "should" do.

NOTES:

_____

_____

_____

_____

_____

_____

_____

_____

QUIT SHOULDERING THE BURDEN

You are not here to be a burden dump. You are here to show that there is another possibility. You are here to lift people up by being high in spirit and heaped in happiness. You are not meant to take their heavy load. You are here to invite them to put it down and leave it. Quit shouldering the burdens, the unhappiness, the grief, the sadness, the anger, and the upset of others. You aren't helping. You are only making you incapable of anything else – like being amazing.

NOTES:

RECOGNIZE WHAT IS MEANINGLESS

All our thoughts, worries, and troubles are meaningless. They don't add any meaning to this world and by continuing to give them credence, we make the world a more meaningless place. What has meaning? Kindness. Generosity. Laughter. Encouragement. Forgiveness. All of these things add meaning to the world and to our lives. Let us give up meaningless for something that has meaning.

NOTES:

RECOGNIZING DIVINE GUIDANCE AND THE IMPOSTERS

How many of us are wanting to do the right thing? The right thing is a judgment. It says if you don't do this "right thing" then you will be wrong. Divine guidance never judges and it never tells you what to do. It never will take away your free will or say it knows better than you. Divine guidance guides. It gives options and possibilities from which you are free to choose. Divine guidance will never say, "You should do this." If you hear a voice telling you what to do, it is an imposter. Don't listen. Instead, go for the non-judgmental kindness of true divine guidance that allows for you and all of your choices.

NOTES:

_____

_____

_____

_____

_____

_____

_____

REFUSING IS NOT CHOOSING

Refusing things is not choosing things. Are you trying to get rid of what is unwanted thinking that once that is gone you will have what you desire? That's not actually true. Instead, what would you like to say yes to? What would you like to add to your life instead of trying to rid your life of? What could you be creating and generating if you stopped refusing its opposite? Say yes to something today and create instead of pushing something away.

NOTES:

RELAX. STUFF HAPPENS

Stuff happens. Stuff that we wish didn't happen, happens. Our first inclination is often to wonder what we did wrong or wonder why we are being punished. You didn't do anything wrong and you are not being punished. Don't make it about you. Just get busy with continuing to create your life as you would like it. Don't let "stuff" stop or derail you from your dreams…and sometimes you might want to ask, "Did this stuff happen to derail me onto a better course?" Nothing is against you. Relax and keep creating.

NOTES:

_____

_____

_____

_____

_____

_____

_____

_____

RELEASE CONTROL

Let your energy go completely out of control! This will give it the freedom to result in something greater and more joyful. You may know the outcome you wish but if you released all conclusion around it, you may find you don't know how much better it could be. Let go and see what happens today!

NOTES:

RELEASE DOUBT

Whenever you are doubtful, you are disregarding your knowing and wisdom. Acknowledge that you do know, even if it is not readily apparent. Often doubt means you are refusing to look at some truth or awareness. What might it be? Most likely it is your greatness and capacity to do anything. Go ahead with certainty and release doubt from your mind. You are amazing and you do know. Do not doubt that. If you allowed yourself to know what you do know, what would it be?

NOTES:

RELEASE STRUGGLE

Somewhere along the line we bought into the idea that struggle is a good thing, or a necessary thing, or the thing that makes everything valuable having gone through it. All of that is a lie. All of it. What are you trying to prove by struggling? Have you proven it? Is it time to let it go? Will you acknowledge it is not your ticket into heaven? Your struggle is not a test and you aren't failing or passing. It is a choice. Release struggle today and let life be easy. Prove to yourself that you earn nothing but grief with struggle.

NOTES:

RELEASE REVENGE

Wherever you said you would get even or you would prove someone wrong, you are sabotaging yourself. You are stuck in the nastiness of hatred and your focus is solely on what you despise. Instead, focus on what you wish to go toward and create. Focus on something else, something better, that will actually create more in the world. Release revenge and you give yourself a chance to create something you really enjoy.

NOTES:

REMOVAL OF THE SHOULDS AND HAVE TOS

What if we removed every "should" we have in our life? Every "I should do this" gone. What if it is just a choice and one not better than the other? What if we removed every "have to" from our lives? Every "I have to do this" gone. What if everything we do or do not do is just a choice and does not require judgment. What might we choose then when the obligation of "I have to" and the judgment of "I should" was no longer there? I wonder?

NOTES:

_____

_____

_____

_____

_____

_____

_____

_____

RIGHTEOUS INDIGNATION IS A KILLER

We go around always looking for the right thing to do and this, more than anything, leads to our downfall. If there is a right, then there is a wrong and you will always be trying to fight or defend for what is right instead of just allowing yourself to be. You are an infinite being which means you are everything in this infinite universe - the right and the wrong. So every time you go for the right only, you lop off half of who you are by dismissing or vilifying the wrong. Kill your righteous indignation today and just be without trying to justify its rightness or wrongness. Just be without judgment. Who might you be if there were no judgments placed upon you? Ah, that feels better.

NOTES:

SAVOURING PLEASURE

To savour pleasure you must surrender to it, be grateful for it, and allow it to be sustained in your life. Will you fully embrace bliss in your life? It's such a strange question, but will you? Or have you decided that you don't have bliss, can't have bliss, and therefore don't need it? Allow the blissfulness and pleasure of being fill you today and savour it.

NOTES:

SELF-RESPECT

Honour and love yourself through healthful actions. Any action, even if done for the good of others, that harms your spirit, is not self-respect. It is manipulation or guilt or actions based on other's opinions of what you should do. Respect and honour your true wants and needs today without being harsh to others. Sometimes that means just saying "I need this and so you will have to do for yourself while I do for myself." Self-respect doesn't mean selfishness. It means honouring you first and that in turn will honour everyone. Be your most fun and easy self today. Honour her or him. Don't worry about those who get their feathers rumpled in the process. They are not honouring you.

NOTES:

SENSITIVITY

You are far more sensitive to energies around you than you may realize. You pick up other people's thoughts and emotions. Instead of trying to juggle the bombardment of fear, worry, and negativity, allow yourself to detach, come back to center with your breath, and take charge once again of your own energetic space. Use your imagination to fill that space with love, faith, calm, and freedom. You are not responsible for other's emotions just because you are aware of them. You are only responsible for your own. Pay attention to your own energy today and stop fighting against others. You will feel the joy that is within you and it will make your day brighter.

NOTES:

SEXY

Bring out your sexiness today. Sexy is a receiving energy. It is an energy that allows and invites the pleasures of the Universe to come to you. How much energy do you put towards destroying your sexiness? How about letting that go? How much energy are you using to block receiving? What if, instead, you were an open invitation to all the pleasure, abundance, and joy the Universe has to offer you? There is no sin in that. Embrace your inner sexy today and receive the joys of this.

NOTES:

SIMPLIFYING YOUR LIFE

It is time to release anything that clutters or complicates your life. By doing this, you will create an energy flow that was not present before. Out with the old and in with the new. Let go of old shoes, clothes, and other items that can be given away. Throw away that which you have never used once in the last 5 years. Let go of outdated thoughts and beliefs that are complicating your life. Think about living and existing simply and enjoying the simple pleasures of life. All that you need will come to you when you need it. If you don't need it now, release it. Then feel the lightness that this brings.

NOTES:

SOMETIMES OTHERS AREN'T AS KIND AS YOU

This is a tough one. We sometimes can not fathom the unkindness that others project at us. It hurts. We feel like the reason they are unkind is because there is something wrong with us. But that's not true. Other's unkindness toward you is about their character, not yours. Anywhere you made their character greater than yours as if they have a right or a necessary responsibility to be unkind to you is a lie. You are hurt because you are kind. That is not a shortcoming. Please be kind to yourself and realize that unkindness is never and has never been greater than kindness for people.

NOTES:

_____

_____

_____

_____

_____

_____

SPACE

When you make yourself space you create space for you to breathe easily, see clearly, and be. Allow your energy to expand out and create space for yourself. Let the molecules know you are here to be in harmony with them and ask how they might contribute to you and your life. When you are space you will not feel trapped or confined or limited. You will find your limitless, infinite capacities to expand and grow. Enjoy!

NOTES:

SPEED UP

In a world where everyone is trying to slow down, do you actually wish things would speed up? What if you allowed yourself to be different from the norm? What if you allowed yourself to be as lightning fast as you are, able to do a hundred million things in a fraction of a second? After a certain age, society tries to slow down. People slow down their life and their body. They become sluggish and a couch potato. Is it time for you to speed up you and your body, and enjoy the thrill of the ride?

NOTES:

_____

_____

_____

_____

_____

_____

_____

_____

SPREAD THE JOY

Where can you use your sparkle to brighten up someone else's day? Sometimes, when we get involved in our own troubles, we forget that we can still make a difference in someone else's life - which is actually the solution to getting out of your doldrums. Look at brightening another's day, making them smile, or lifting up their world with your awesomeness. You may find that joy spills right back into your own world.

NOTES:

_____

_____

_____

_____

_____

_____

_____

_____

_____

START DELEGATING

It is time to start setting boundaries with yourself and others and ask others to do what they can do for themselves. You don't need to be at the beck and call of everyone else's ego demands. If it fills your heart and feels good to help someone, then do. But if it feels like a burden, then you must delegate that responsibility back to them by gently but firmly saying no. You don't have to do it all. You don't have to walk this path alone. So, free yourself from burdens and start giving them back to their owners with love.

NOTES:

_____

_____

_____

_____

_____

_____

_____

STAY ON POINT

We often cloud our desires and everyday activities with excuses, distractions, and justifications. All of these are time wasters. They also keep you from actually creating with clarity and efficiency. Keep your eye on the prize with unwavering focus and faith. No excuses. No distractions. No justifications.

NOTES:

STOP BEING NORMAL

Normal means you are like the majority. You aren't and you never will be. You are unique unto yourself - one of a kind - NOT alone - just precious. This difference is what makes you valuable. Stop trying to be normal. You feel like you are failing because you are. You are failing the normal test. You aren't normal and never will be so you might as well be you and discover the pricelessness that brings and celebrate acing the unique test.

NOTES:

_____

_____

_____

_____

_____

_____

_____

_____

STOP RUSHING

How often do we rush around, getting things done, and not aware of what else is going on around us? When you find yourself going non-stop, maybe let yourself stop, breathe, take everything in, and know that it's all going to get done (even if you don't know how). Sometimes, allowing yourself to be aware of your life lets you enjoy it. Just a thought.

NOTES:

_____

_____

_____

_____

_____

_____

_____

_____

_____

STOP THE CYCLE

Whenever you determine that you are or someone is undeserving, then you perpetuate a cycle of undeservingness, unworthiness, and lack. Be the first to break the cycle. Stop denying the undeserving and allow for everything and anything with anyone and everyone. You will not lose doing this. Not only do you win, but so does everyone else. What commitments do you have to winning the game of judging who is deserving that keeps you in the perpetual cycle of playing with lack? Are you willing to stop policing who deserves what and start blessing everyone with abundance, including yourself?

NOTES:

_____

_____

_____

_____

_____

_____

_____

STOP THINKING

When you try to figure things out, you overthink. Overthinking leads to frustration. Stop and ask a question. What else is possible? What is my next move that will bring me joy? How does it get any better than this? Sit in question and leave thinking be for awhile. Thinking only rehashes what you already know. Questions allow for something new and better to show up. Go to question, breathe, and leave it be for awhile. You do not need to do anything this second. Wait with question.

NOTES:

_____

_____

_____

_____

_____

_____

_____

_____

STOP ANALYZING FEAR

How many of us use fear as a reason to not do something? It is not a reason. It is an excuse. Let's stop giving fear any validity. When we no longer make fear part of our decision making, a lot blocks and obstacles fall away. Perhaps they were never there until we entertained fear. It's not that we have to make the fear go away. It's just that we must not let it be in control or ever have a say in whether we go ahead or not. If it won't leave, let it sit in the back seat, or better yet, the trunk. It doesn't get to give directions.

NOTES:

_____

_____

_____

_____

_____

_____

_____

_____

SURPLUS ENERGY

Most of the time we operate with the energy of lack. Is it time to change your energy to surplus? Having more than enough? Do you allow for surplus? Do you open your arms to more than you think you need? Surplus energy allows for more - more to have, more to give, more for all including you. Surplus means you won't run out. Shift your energy to being the energy of surplus today instead of being the energy of lack. See what happens.

NOTES:

TENACITY AND DETERMINATION

Change starts with you. Sometimes you must pull on your gifts of tenacity and determination to see things through. If you refuse to waver in your quest, determined for change to happen, it will. You won't have to fight for long. Just keep seeing yourself past the things that pull you back or distract you. You have power within you. Use it. Stop pretending you don't.

NOTES:

THE ASK

It may seem obvious, but if you want something, you must ask for it with your energy. Nothing actually comes from other people. We think it does. "Mom, can I have a cookie?" We are brought up believing other people, like our parents, need to say yes or no to our requests. But it is our energy that determines the answer of what we will receive. So when you ask for the cookie, are you being the energy of "I'm getting the cookie, oh, yeah!" or are you being, "They don't want to give me a cookie. Oh, woe is me"? Start paying attention to what you are asking for with your energy. Change your energy and you will change the answer.

NOTES:

_____

_____

_____

_____

_____

_____

_____

_____

THE PROBLEM WITH YOU/ME IS

You are invited to challenge any statement that begins with these 5 words. What if the only problem is that you believe there is a problem? The moment you think there is a problem with you, you summon Universal energies to create a problem so that you can prove that indeed, you are right, there is a problem. Challenge any existing problems that you have already identified by asking "What if this isn't a problem?" and "What if there is no problem with me?" Stop needing to be right about your problems and instead entertain that you are completely wrong about being a problem. What if there is absolutely nothing wrong with you? Or anyone else? What if you actually entertained the truth of that?

NOTES:

_____

_____

_____

_____

_____

_____

_____

THERE IS ALWAYS ENOUGH TIME

You fool yourself by constantly saying that there never is enough time. There is. You also never fool yourself when you say that you can make time. Have you ever noticed when you choose to do something, the time is available? Not enough time is an excuse people make to not choose or to suffer. What would you do if you had the time for it? Choose it and the time will appear.

NOTES:

_____

_____

_____

_____

_____

_____

_____

_____

_____

THERE IS NOTHING WRONG WITH YOU

When we set out on a journey to better ourselves, sometimes we decide what we are is wrong and needing to be fixed. Not so. You can change. You can make new choices, but those things don't make you more right or "fixed". They just make things different. It is difficult to create with ease and move forward when you are constantly believing you have a broken part that needs to be fixed. You don't.

NOTES:

_____

_____

_____

_____

_____

_____

_____

THE STORY CALLED YOUR LIFE

You are living the story called your life and it is totally a work in progress. Would you be willing for it not to be the fixed outcome you've already decided? Would you allow for a happy middle and end and for it to be a story of ease, magic, and wonder? Would you allow yourself to re-write it and envision a completely unknown ending that carries all the possibilities and choices an infinite universe can offer? Will you choose the most unbelievable elements and scenarios that would be SO MUCH FUN? Don't relive the same old story. Try a new one that is constantly changing, evolving, getting better and better and never, ever limiting you but instead always creating more. What might that be like?

NOTES:

_____

_____

_____

_____

_____

_____

_____

TIME

It is time to let go of time and allow for instantaneous results. What if it doesn't have to take years or months for you to release that thought or belief that has been plaguing you since you can remember? What if it doesn't have to take two weeks to gain the clarity of the decision you wish to make? What if you could have it now? Isn't it time to open to the possibility? Isn't it time to remove time from the equation? Then whatever shows up isn't bound by a timeline. This doesn't mean everything will be instantaneous, but it does mean that what could be now you no longer have to wait for. What if? Remove time from all your equations and just see what happens....

NOTES:

TIME TO MOVE ON

What have you trapped yourself in? What mood doesn't ever seem to escape you? It is time to move on. It is time to leave the pain, suffering, and upset and simply move on. Let go of needing to figure out why it happened or how you could have made it different. Move on. Get on with living a happy life. Sometimes we just have to acknowledge things didn't happen the way we would have liked, and we can move forward creating something better, instead of lamenting and wallowing in the past. It is time to move on.

NOTES:

_____

_____

_____

_____

_____

_____

_____

_____

TOMORROW IS YOUR LAST DAY

Imagine tomorrow is your last day on earth. What do you wish to do today? What are the things you want to do, but no longer have the time for? Do you have any unfulfilled business? Get busy filling it. Get busy telling people how much they mean to you. When you think about your life this way, you won't waste time. So get on with it. What needs your attention now?

NOTES:

TREAT OTHERS LIKE YOU WISH TO BE TREATED, NOT HOW YOU WERE TREATED

We often treat others in the same manner in which we have been treated instead of the way we wish to be treated. This just keeps the cycle of unkindness and abuse going. If you wish for change then a change in you is required. Could this be it? We mimic what we have experienced as if experiencing it somehow made it right. You can be the change you are seeking. Treat others like you wish you would be treated. You have it in you, and when you do, you find that others treat you that way too.

NOTES:

_____

_____

_____

_____

_____

_____

TURN NECESSITY INTO PRIORITY

We make many things we wish to be priorities in our life necessary and in doing so, trap ourselves by creating no choice. When something is a necessity, there is no choice. You must do or have it. When something is a priority you choose to make it high on your list to pay attention to, which not only gives you choice, but complete control over what choices you make. For example, is it a necessity to go to work or a priority? Which makes you feel better? Knowing you have the choice not to go to work, makes you feel less resentful about going because you recognize you are choosing it. Insert whatever you feel resentment or trapped about, recognize how you have made it a necessity, then make it a priority. Then you will have your choice and your life back. Have fun with this today! In fact, why not make it a priority?

NOTES:

VALIDATION COMES FROM YOU

In this crazy world where we keep seeking the validation and approval of others, we only need give it to ourselves and everyone else's opinions becomes irrelevant. Ask, "Where am I seeking validation?" Get the energy of that and consciously choose to allow for whatever it is you are seeking approval on. Allow for it to be. Approve of yourself as you are; approve of your hopes and dreams today, and you just might find they all can now come true because they no longer caught up in the red tape of a validation process. You don't need permission to make your dreams come true.

NOTES:

_____

_____

_____

_____

_____

_____

_____

VICTORY!

Your prayers have been heard and answered. Have faith. So often, we become impatient. We believe if we don't see evidence of our prayers manifesting, then they aren't. Not true. Much goes on behind the scenes before the show can be put on. Celebrate. All is happening as it should. Have faith that victory is soon near. Don't let your impatience spoil or delay the victory. Keep telling yourself it is happening! Instead of fear and anxiety, feel excited. This will make your day better and your prayers come to fruition quicker.

NOTES:

VISION OF YOUR FUTURE

Where are you headed? What future have you created? Are you looking forward, anticipating the next adventure? Or are you looking backward to the past? When we don't look to the future and acknowledge it's brighter than today, then we will feel lifeless, gloomy, or in despair. When we look to the past, we feel like we have to correct a bunch of mistakes, which we don't. Have a vision of your future and keep your eye upon it so that it may guide you to it. See your life as getting better and better, because it can and it is.

NOTES:

_____

_____

_____

_____

_____

_____

_____

_____

WAITING FOR SOMETHING BETTER

The best way to get to something better is to choose something right now. This will get you moving to the next choice which will be better and so on. Waiting for something better leaves you constantly and eternally waiting and wondering why it isn't happening for you. By waiting it is like hoping to jump to the top of the mountain from where you are. You don't have to be at the top of the mountain - just take a step closer to it and then the next will appear. Eventually you get there. Wait and you may wait forever.

NOTES:

WHAT ARE YOU ROMANTICIZING?

Romantic notions can trap us from seeing the truth and moving on. Have you ever had a relationship from the past that you still think of? Ever wonder of what might have been? Or about the one who got away? Living in the past doesn't allow you to enjoy the present or the future. Let go of your romantic notions that true love wins in the end or that Prince Charming comes to save you. Create your own happy ending by letting go of what should have been and acknowledging what was with gratitude and acceptance. Then you will be free to move forward.

NOTES:

WHAT ARE YOU SO AFRAID TO LOSE THAT IT CONTROLS YOU?

The moment you realize that this thing that you are afraid to lose, whatever it is, doesn't hold a candle to the creative power of you, you will be free of its hold on you. Then you can have all that you wish. Would you be willing to let go of wealth, fame, poverty, validation, a job? What controls you? Be willing to let it go and you are free. You also may find that it comes to you more easily when you aren't trying to back it into a wall and cage it. Face what controls you and be willing to say goodbye to it. Never give yourself up for something. You always lose that way.

NOTES:

_____

_____

_____

_____

_____

_____

_____

WHAT FAMILY ROLE ARE YOU PLAYING?

What's the role of you in your family? Is that role working for you or limiting you? Would you be willing to give it up? Would you be willing to no longer be the black sheep, the harmonizer, the spoiled one, daddy's favourite, the one who does it all because no one else will, or whatever role it is you are playing? Would that create more or less in your world? You do not have to be what your family expects you to be. You can be you. If they don't expect that, then they really aren't being kind to you or them, are they?

NOTES:

_____

_____

_____

_____

_____

_____

_____

WHAT IF CHEAP CHEAPENS?

By always choosing the cheapest to save money, you actually may be cheapening yourself and devaluing you and your world. Where have you committed to poverty? Are you willing to now choose something greater? Are you willing to honour what would bring you the most joy and choose it even if the price tag attached is higher than others around you? It's not about choosing the most expensive item. It's about choosing what will bring you the greatest joy and contribution to your life. That may mean it is the cheapest one. It may mean it is the most expensive. It may mean somewhere in between. Where is the most joy and contribution? Go with that and you will never feel cheap nor will you ever cheapen you or your life again.

NOTES:

_____

_____

_____

_____

_____

_____

WHAT IS POSSIBLE HERE?

When you have exhausted all the possibilities it is time to ask "What else is possible here?" We get in our heads that we know all the possibilities and that we have finite resources to work with. What is the point of living in this infinite Universe if we don't access what it has to offer? And boy oh boy does it have things, unimaginable resources, to offer. Ask, then put down your righteous indignation that you know everything (tough for some of us) and open to receive something completely different. And then do it again.

NOTES:

WHAT QUESTION ARE YOU ASKING?

The questions we ask get specific results. It is important to pay attention to the questions we ask. For example, questions like "Why does this always happen to me?" will only get you more results of that horrible thing happening to you so that you can figure out why. A question of "How do I change this?" is better. A question of "What possibilities can come to me now that will bring me joy?" is even better. Think about what you're putting out there. Is it getting you the results that you desire? And, how can they get even better?

NOTES:

_____

_____

_____

_____

_____

_____

_____

_____

WHAT'S YOUR GO-TO PROTECTION STANCE?

Many of us try to protect ourselves with anger. Feeling like someone is challenging you, you become angry to ward off their opposition. Others become passive-aggressively silent and walled. Some go to tears as a distraction method. Some use insults and meanness. Some go straight to violence or self-destructive behaviours like drugs, alcohol, or reckless driving. Only problem is none of these protect you and they certainly don't make your life better. Would you be willing to drop your protection strategy for knowing you are ok and that you don't have to judge or oppose opposition? When you do this, it has nothing to stick to and falls away. Just a suggestion you might like to try someday.

NOTES:

_____

_____

_____

_____

_____

_____

WHAT YOU ARE AFRAID OF IS A FALSE THREAT

There is never any need for you to be afraid to make a choice or do something you want to do. The Universe has your back. Move forward fearlessly without troubles in your heart or fear in your soul. Anything you think that threatens you is a false threat. It is designed to control you into inaction. Nothing is more powerful than your choice to create. Go ahead and be you.

NOTES:

_____

_____

_____

_____

_____

_____

_____

_____

WHEN WILL YOU BE HAPPY?

Is it when you have more money? Is it when you find a soul mate? When you get a better job? When you retire? How about now? What if you didn't have to wait? How long are you going to wait to be happy? What if outside conditions have nothing to do with your ability to choose happiness right now?

NOTES:

WHERE DO I GO FROM HERE?

Whenever you find yourself mired in a past event, wondering how you could have done things differently or thinking about how upset you are it happened, it is time to leave the past and ask, "Where do I go from here?" Get focused on moving forward and leaving what you are thinking about behind. What's done is done. It is time to create something better, and that won't happen if you continually live in a moment of the past.

NOTES:

WHO ARE YOUR ACCUSERS?

When you feel backed into a corner, or simply unable to do or be what you would like, ask who are your accusers? Whoever they may be, they are not the Universe, or God, or anything that has any real power over you. The Universe will never judge you. It will never accuse you as if you are doing something wrong. Whoever is accusing you, release. If you are accusing you, cut yourself the slack and let that go. In the truth of consciousness, you are always allowed for and never condemned.

NOTES:

WHO'S NOT LOVING YOU?

If you don't feel loved, or you feel that you are not enough, then it is solely because you are not loving you, nor being kind to you, nor acknowledging all the wonders that you are. You may refute claims of your lovability by giving yourself examples of how you don't measure up, and that is more non-loving unkindness that you are directing at yourself. Will you stop with the unkindness directed at you by you? No one else has to agree. No one but you. The irony is once you do, everyone else will too, or you won't care that they don't - because you will be loved - by you. Please, do yourself this one kindness today and just be loving to you in every way.

NOTES:

_____

_____

_____

_____

_____

_____

_____

_____

WILL YOU ALLOW FOR THE MIRACLE?

Will you allow for the miracle in order for change to occur? Will you let go of your righteous indignation that it can't happen? Will you soften to receive it? Will you open to the possibility that miracles can and do happen? They happen everyday. Not because others are more deserving than you, but because those who receive them open to receive them and allow for the possibility of the change to exist. Think I'm wrong? You're right. Think I'm right? You're right. Who cares what I think? What you think is the most important thing. Do you think miracles can happen for you?

NOTES:

_____

_____

_____

_____

_____

_____

_____

_____

WINNERS, LOSERS, AND THE ONES YOU DON'T COUNT

Winners are those people you think are so great that if you could be in their crowd it would elevate your status. Losers are those people who would give up their lives to be in your presence because they think you'd elevate their status. The ones you don't count are the ones you can always count on. They don't elevate you and you don't elevate them, but they will contribute to your life and, ironically, they are the people you can always count on. Always give more attention to the ones that don't count, because really they count the most.

NOTES:

_____

_____

_____

_____

_____

_____

_____

WITHIN YOU, AS YOU

Your creative power lies within you, as you. Are you being what you would like your life to be? If you wish for a big life, are you being a big energy? If you wish for a happy life, are you being happy? When we become reactive to the things around us, we end up with an unfocused life at the mercy of anyone and anything around us. There is no direction or power in that. Remember, your life is created from within you, as you. What do you need to be to create the life you wish for? That's the way to make it happen.

NOTES:

WONDERFUL SURPRISES

The Universe is full of wonderful surprises and is wondering when you are going to gleefully allow them to pop into your life. When we think the world is harsh or rough or mean or wrong or screwed up or against you, then the Universe must return that same energy to you to prove your belief. What if the Universe is kind and fun and joyful and silly and generous and exciting? When you believe in the truth of that then the Universe must return that energy to you. It will do so in the most amazing surprising ways that you could never imagine on your own. What if we stopped trying to tell the Universe how to surprise us (which really isn't a surprise at all), and allow it to delight us in the way it knows best? What wonderful surprises may crop up for you I wonder?

NOTES:

WORTH WAITING FOR

Just because what you want hasn't shown up yet doesn't mean it's not coming. Patience, please. Trust and faith, please! We sometimes decide that things have to happen on our schedule, but the Universe works with divine time and it often does not match our 9-5, overly planned, overly regimented, ego-driven schedules. Relax. If it's not here, something better is coming. Everything that makes your heart sing or your soul soar is worth waiting for. Stop trying to push it, control it, manhandle the outcome, and basically ruin the miracle that could be yours. Have patience, breathe, and relax. Your dreams are coming. Keep dreaming them. Keep believing in them.

NOTES:

_____

_____

_____

_____

_____

_____

_____

WRITE DOWN YOUR THOUGHTS AND FEELINGS

Sometimes it is difficult to understand what is truly going on within. By writing out your thoughts and feelings you provide an outlet for them that is safe and effective. Blow up at the page; it will not judge you. Put your tears on the lines; they will not mock you. Accept that there are issues that need releasing, and let them out on paper. Once you do, you will immediately feel better. You will gain access to divine guidance to assist you. Write it all out. If you are afraid someone else may read it, then burn it. Give it to the Universe to dispel and cleanse. Take time to do this today, and you will feel lighter and more equipped to handle your day. Don't delay. Do it now.

NOTES:

_____

_____

_____

_____

_____

YOU ARE A CONTRIBUTION

Ever feel useless, unwanted, unneeded, or unnecessary? Then you have not acknowledged the contribution you are and can be. This must start with you. Sometimes jumping in and getting your hands dirty is the contribution, but often it is just standing aside and wishing someone well. Make no mistake, you are a contribution to this world or you wouldn't be in it. Acknowledge it. Own it. Be it. Be what you are.

NOTES:

YOU ARE FEARLESS

You are an infinite being. Would an infinite being ever be afraid? No. So why are you? Perhaps you are not. Perhaps the fear you feel doesn't belong to you. Ask, "Truth, am I really afraid? Or, am I just aware of other people's fears of the choices I wish to make?" You are not afraid. You are fearless. You know it when you are being honest with yourself. Whatever fear is stopping you is not yours - bust through and never stop living!

NOTES:

YOU ARE NOT SEPARATE FROM SOURCE

Whatever it is that you desire, you are not separate from its Source. We are all connected as One. Its Source is your Source. The Source resides within you, as you. Open to it being a given that you have and can have anything and everything. Nothing is off limits. And Source shall never condemn you or accuse you for your desire or for the choice to have your desire. Since you are not separate, to condemn you would condemn itself. Stop condemning you and pretending you are separate from the infinite Source. Instead, keep thanking Source for its abundance. Gratitude opens the doors to having.

NOTES:

_____

_____

_____

_____

_____

_____

_____

YOU ARE OK

You No matter how messed up, screwed up, lost, or broken you think you are, you are going to be ok. You are ok. This will pass and things will come and go. Through it all, you are ok, and you're going to be ok. Relax. Breathe. Trust in you. You are ok.

NOTES:

YOU ARE VALUABLE

Have you made yourself the most valuable product in your world? If you are not, then something is always going to take priority over your special contribution and greatness you have come to share with this world. Anytime you make yourself less than anything, you devalue you. Making yourself valuable does not mean you become a superior, egotistical ogre. It means you come to a place of pure gratitude and appreciation for who you are and are then able to spread that gratitude and appreciation to all. What would it take to make yourself the most valuable product in your world today without diminishing anything else?

NOTES:

YOU CAN ASK FOR ANYTHING

You ask with your energy and you can ask for anything. When your energy is saying "I'm having that!" it's going to have it. But so often we don't do this with our energy. Instead, we say, "I can't have that even though I'd like it." So say yes to things you previously thought you "couldn't" have. Just open to the possibility. What haven't you been asking for that if you just said yes to, would open the door to it coming into your life? Be brave. Ask for anything.

NOTES:

YOU CAN DO IT

Don't let doubts, fears, or disappointments get you down. The past does not equal the future unless you decide it has to be that way. Create something new that is different from your past. You wish to and you can do it. Stay strong in your resolve to make change and know you have more than enough ability to make that happen. You can do it! The only question left is "Will you?"

NOTES:

YOU CAN GET SH!T DONE

Acknowledge the massive ability you have to get stuff done. You probably have labelled yourself a control freak and made yourself wrong for it, but part of that is your ability to say, "This gets done NOW" and you can make that happen faster than anyone else around you. That's a gift and a talent and you own it. SO OWN IT. What other gifts and talents do you have that you have put a negative label on and made yourself wrong for? Hmmm. Now, go get some sh!t done!

NOTES:

_____

_____

_____

_____

_____

_____

_____

_____

YOU CAN'T FIX ANYONE

We are powerful creators of our own lives. When we decide something is going to work for us, it will work for us. When we decide nothing seems to work for us, then nothing will seem to work for us. The person is the creator. You can't fix them. You can only believe in them and see them as choosing to be whole and well. Whoever you are trying to fix, stop. What happens when you try to fix someone who doesn't want it or hasn't asked for it is that they block themselves away from receiving even further. It makes it worse. Back off and believe in them. That can work miracles.

NOTES:

_____

_____

_____

_____

_____

_____

_____

YOU CREATED THIS SITUATION AND YOU HAVE THE POWER TO CHANGE IT

You have all the power in the world to change you. All it requires is to change your mind. Where are you making yourself so vehemently right that you can't change your mind? That is what needs changing. Where are you trying desperately to make others wrong or to change them? Stop and work with yourself. Change comes from within - not without. You have the power within you. You can do this.

NOTES:

_____

_____

_____

_____

_____

_____

_____

_____

YOU DON'T HAVE TO FIGURE EVERYTHING OUT

Let the Universe handle the figuring. Your job is to stay in gratitude of the possibility of things being created. Your job is to stay light and happy and assured of wonderful outcomes. Your job is to have fun. When you try to figure things out you only feel doubtful, unsure, and in the dark. Stop figuring. Stop doing the Universe's job and get busy with your own - gratitude and enjoyment.

NOTES:

_____

_____

_____

_____

_____

_____

_____

_____

_____

YOU'RE ON THE RIGHT PATH

The Universe says keep going and doing what you're doing because it is working! Doesn't matter whether you are in the flow or on the rocks; keep moving forward. You are being guided in the right direction. Life is bumpy. Enjoy the ride. You are on the right path. If life is smooth, enjoy that too. Keep it going for as long as you will allow. You are on the right path. You are getting there, so relax. Celebrate! Rejoice! The GPS is working and it says, "Destination straight ahead." The only question is, once you get there, "Where to next?" Enjoy the journey, baby!

NOTES:

_____

_____

_____

_____

_____

_____

_____

YOU ROCK

It is time to pat yourself on the back and acknowledge how awesome you are. Don't wait for some big accomplishment before you do it. Do it now and always and you will be able to accomplish more. Acknowledge the greatness of you instead of hiding, denying, or defending against it. You are an awesome being full of magic and wonder and joy. You ROCK. Don't ever forget it. And tell yourself often!

NOTES:

YOUTHFUL WISDOM

We often associate wisdom with old age, but what if our youth holds more wisdom than we ever gave it credit? What if youth holds the wisdom of vitality, joy, laughter, and carefree living? Do you remember your youth and how things seemed simpler and easier then? What did you know then that you still know but decided not to know because you are too old for that now? Bring back your youthful wisdom. It never left and it never aged. How young and wise can you be today?

NOTES:

_____

_____

_____

_____

_____

_____

_____

_____

ABOUT THE AUTHOR

Fay Thompson is a Perspectives Coach, international speaker, and an Access Consciousness® Certified Facilitator. She also is the founder and Editor-in-Chief of Big Moose Publishing. Fay spends her days writing, editing, coaching individuals and businesses, and facilitating workshops. Her aim is to empower each person to realize their immense creative capacity and their ability to change anything into something greater or different.

Fay resides in Saskatchewan, Canada with her dazzling husband, two gorgeous children, loving dog, Elsa, and playful cat, Comet.

To find out more about Fay and her work, or to book a coaching session or speaking engagement, visit www.faythompson.com. If you are interested in publishing, visit www.bigmoosepublishing.com.

You can also follow her on:

Facebook	www.facebook.com/faythompsoninspires
Instagram	www.instagram.com/faythompsoninspires

www.ingramcontent.com/pod-product-compliance
Lightning Source LLC
Chambersburg PA
CBHW030904080526
44589CB00010B/144